THE
CHURCH
AND
THE
LAITY

FROM
NEWMAN
TO
VATICAN II

the church and the laity

JEAN GUITTON

ALBA HOUSE
a division of St. Paul Publications
Staten Island, N.Y.

Translated by Malachy Gerard Carroll
Original title L'Eglise et les Laïcs published by Desclée de Brouwer

Nihil Obstat:

James F. Rigney, S.T.D.

Censor Librorum

Imprimatur:

✠ Francis Cardinal Spellman

Archbishop of New York

December 10, 1964

The Nihil Obstat and Imprimatur are official declarations that a book or pamphlet is free of doctrinal or moral error. No implication is contained therein that those who have granted the Nihil Obstat and Imprimatur agree with the contents, opinions or statements expressed.

Library of Congress Catalog Card Number 65-15730

Designed, printed and bound in the U.S.A. by the Pauline Fathers and Brothers as part of their publishing apostolate. They were founded to spread Christ's message by means of the press, radio, motion pictures and television. A brochure on the Paulines can be obtained by sending a card to: Society of St. Paul, Vocation Office. 2187 Victory Blvd., Staten Island, N.Y. 10314 - tel. Area 212 - GI-2-0047

Contents

Preface

"He (Sir James Stephen) wanted from me a new philosophy. He wanted Christianity developed to meet the age. . . ." Letter to Rev. R. H. Froude: January 28, 1836.

Drama of 'The Rambler'

Recently, while browsing through the letters of Madame de Sévigné, I came across this astonishing passage:

"I am reading the book *Arianisme* and I like neither the author nor the style. However, the history is admirable: it is that of the whole world; it extends to everything; it has springs to set all powers in motion. The spirit of Arius is amazing, and to see this heresy spread by everyone! Nearly all the Bishops were of it. Only St. Athanasius upheld the Divinity of Christ." (July 14, 1680).

It would be hard to better this as focusing the interest of a book on the Arians. And if Madame de Sévigné had been able to read Newman's "The Arians of the Fourth Century," she might well have expressed herself in the same way, though hardly about the author and the style.

––––––

When the Vatican Council was recessed, I took the opportunity of returning to my intellectual origins and sources: I immersed myself in the Newman Studies which had enchanted my youth and given my life its axis. I have a great love for Newman, and every time I return to him, I gain a fresher and more intimate understanding of Catholicism.

Though Newman is not a philosopher or an exegete, though we look to him neither for logic (in the scholastic sense) nor for a coherent system of thought, though he disconcerted the Latin mind, I find him incomparable among the modern masters. He affects me deeply, both in my thought and in the sensitivity of my responses to life. Reading his works, I can see all things in harmony: the Mysteries of the Faith known in themselves through shadows and figures and motivated by the developments of history, and the mysteries of my intimate and personal life. Every old problem is seen in a new light when it passes through the Newman prism. Newman's style is clear music, at once Attic and English, as though Oxford had become Greece. Furthermore, at a remove of some hundred years, he was a good prophet of what we are now witnessing; he was an excellent adapter of the Church to its future. Reading Newman, I have the impression of the ever fresh youthfulness of the Church. I notice the fact, paradoxical but certainly verified during recent decades, that Catholicism alone is fully capable of preparing humanity for the future pattern of human life. I cherish a wish to see Newman raised to the greatest of all honors, and I can still hear the soft firm intonation of Pope Pius XII, when he reassured me in these words: "Have no doubt of it, Monsieur Guitton, Newman will one day be a Doctor of the Church."

Since I was fifteen, Newman has been my guide to all truth. My mother had given him to me to be my model, after she had read the book, which still holds its place, by Lucie Félix-Faure Goyau.

"He has a vigor, elasticity and what may be called

sunniness of mind," Newman says about St. John Chrysostom. The words are an even more apt description of
Newman himself.

But let us return to "The Arians of the Fourth Century,"
his first book. Let us take a retrospective look at it in the
indirect light of the Vatican Council.

Newman's book could have been subtitled, "The History of a Council." It is the *full* history of the Council of
Nicaea, being less concerned with the Council itself than
with what preceded and especially what followed it. The
long post-history of Nicaea is indeed dramatic. Opposition
to the *de fide* dogmatic definition of Nicaea called in question the work of that Council. And Semi-Arianism, more
difficult than Arianism to distinguish from orthodoxy,
tended to cause the faith of Nicaea to vanish in evasive
subtleties.

Like everything with the human element, a Council is
subject to the laws of time and to the vicissitudes of freedom. As the contemporary St. Jerome had clearly seen,
and as Newman was to point out so dramatically, there
was a surprising moment in the Fourth Century when the
majority of the Bishops wavered in the Faith, which was
integrally defended only by the Pope, by Bishop Athanasius and by the laity.

Surprising is the recurrent key word of this book. It is
possible, therefore, that the laity helped to save the Faith!
This is what astonished the young Newman when he was
studying the history of the Arians.

Discovery of 'The Rambler'

When, about 1924, I decided to write a thesis on Newman, I devoted myself entirely to the subject. One of the
first objectives of my prolonged study in the British Mu-

seum was to discover his little known, marginal perhaps, unsigned writings. I knew from Thureau-Dangin that the Cardinal suppressed an article which had appeared in a review after his conversion. Newman, who loved to collect together the smallest matters concerning his personal life, who assembled his letters, who published his *Opera omnia* in his lifetime, would nonetheless never republish this article. I was intrigued by this, and I can remember my excitement when one of the excellent British Museum attendants placed on my table a volume of *The Rambler*. It contained, if I am not mistaken, a badly printed and unsigned article, but I read that article as though it were a sacred text. My thesis was about *Development*, but I could hardly use this highly theological, very learned, extremely personal study. I thought I should respect the Cardinal's own desire as regards this article. However, I included in my book this comment which no one particularly noticed:

"Newman's orthodoxy was defended by Pius X in his letter to Bishop O'Dwyer of Limerick (March 10, 1908): *Profecto in tanta lucubrationum ejus copia, quidpiam reperiri potest, quod ab usitate theologorum ratione alienum videatur, nihil potest quod de ipsius fide suspicionem afferat* (*Epistola "Tuum illud opusculum"* ad Romanum Episcopum *Limiricensem*). Newman's opinions about Modernism could be gathered from his conference, *A Form of Infidelity of the Day* (*Idea*, 381-404). In the Catholic period of his life, I know of only one occasion when he could reproach himself with an unbecoming tone. Newman had often expressed the idea that, without the Christian people (*the laity*) the Christian faith after the Council of Nicaea would have been in the utmost danger, because the Bishops, with some illustrious exceptions, were very feeble in upholding that Council. He had developed this point in an article headed *On Consulting the faithful in Matters of Doctrine* which appeared in *The Rambler* (July 1859), and was later summarized in Note V appended to the definitive edition of his work, *"The Arians of the Fourth Century."* Newman, however, decided to omit the last phrase of his 1859 article: *"a fides implicita* in her word (i.e. the word of the *Ecclesia docens*), which in the educated classes will terminate in indifference, and in the poorer in superstition." (*The Rambler, loc. cit.,* p. 230).

After that, I thought no more about *The Rambler* until the Vatican Council, and especially its second session, gave a new relevance to this article which is so characteristic of the method, the courage and the prophetic spirit of Newman. It leads one to reflect about the work of the Holy Ghost in the Church through a faithful laity.

The Newman article is not unknown in France: thanks to Father Congar, it has been judiciously included in *Pensées sur l'Eglise de J. H. Newman* (1956). Geoffrey Chapman has republished the article (London, 1961), with a very full and fine introduction by John Coulson which can be taken as the last word on the subject. There can be no point in going over the ground again.

Anyhow, my approach is quite different. I want to apply to this text what Pascal calls "the order of charity," which consists "in digression about each point to which one returns at the end to show that it remains the same." This leads me to consider the Newman text as a kind of precious stone with many facets in which several problems are reflected. At times, I shall study it from the point of view of Newman himself, and I shall direct upon it certain rays derived from Newman and from what I know about his story and his mystery; at times I shall consider and re-think it in the perspective of the Vatican Council. I shall seek help from him in my effort to define the place of the laity in the Church.

Newman and 'The Rambler' Article.

I begin with the most difficult aspect of this matter, but one which has interested me so much in connection with the saints and spiritual persons. I mean the attempt to trace and to understand the curve of their destiny, and that amalgam of Providential Love, of fortuitous events, of free acts, which is called predestination. This is an unfathomable mystery, of course, but a mystery of which one may catch some refracted ray, through the guidance of St. Augustine in his *Confessions* (or through Newman, a second Augustine, in his *Apologia*). The Rambler article gives us such a glimpse.

When one carefully studies the inner pattern of a life, one notices that it is often determined by one circumstance. This can be a very minor action, a choice buried in our deepest being, which has led us to sacrifice our ease in order *to risk* something, or conversely to embrace our ease when we should have acted, to choose silence when we should have spoken out. We can never tell when this furtive free will action may occur—an action which, while without apparent effect at the actual moment, gives to a whole portion of our life its curve, its color, its axis, its irreversibility. (We never know whether some day we will still be called on to sacrifice our ease and our new assurances). *To be at ease is to be unsafe,* says Newman.

Newman's decision, in May 1859, to publish in *The Rambler* his article about the laity, may well have been the *meritorious* act of the second part of his life. Reading his letters, I noticed that Newman venerated saints, such as his beloved St. Philip Neri, who died at an advanced age; he was keenly aware that advanced age seeks comfort, and, when faced with troubling perspectives, is only too ready to hearken to the whisper: 'You are not to concern yourself about that.'

By this study, which he knew would be ill received at Rome, Newman reinforced his morale and his conception of Catholic honor.

He had proved to himself that the Roman Church was the one true Church. More than any other Christian of his day, he had shown the value he placed on the difference between that Church and all other Churches. He had sacrificed everything—honors, tender friendships, natural ties—to the *little difference* which separated the Anglican Church from the Church of Rome. But the principle which had led him to this total sacrifice (a sacrifice more difficult perhaps than the quickly terminated sacrifice of martyrdom) was the principle of being true to himself, the principle of fidelity to what he held to be in conformity with historical truth. It was impossible for him to say that what is, is not; or what is not, is. If conflict arose between his duties towards authority and his duties towards himself, he would attempt to reconcile these opposing demands somewhat in the manner of the mystics who, despite confusion and appearances, would never accept that light can be opposed to light. And, if necessary, in his full maturity and with the peace of a harbor at last reached after many storms, he would sacrifice himself again; without abandoning his peace, his Mother the Church and obedience to her disciplines, he would put out again into the waters of suspicion and silence.

Such was the axis of one who, twenty years later and by then a Cardinal, was to reply to Gladstone's accusation of servility by saying that if he could propose two toasts at a banquet he would drink first to his conscience and then to the Pope.

One can see how very much was involved, from the moral point of view, in that apparently small decision to publish an article.

It must be remembered that Newman—so sensitive to abuse and naturally a solitary person, perhaps indeed somewhat relishing the misunderstandings which enabled him to fight alone—was twice in situations of non-conformity. On both occasions he fought, and on both occasions he was led to break with his companions at arms. As a member of the Anglican Church, he fought with his friends at Oxford to awaken in the Clergy the slumbering sense of their priesthood. He was suspected, then condemned, by Anglican hierarchic authority. After his conversion, he took up the same arms to awaken in the Catholic Church the slumbering significance of the laity. Again he was misunderstood in his day, and justified only by time.

The tone of *The Rambler* article was challenging, its language sometimes imprecise and not conforming to the usual technical vocabulary approved for such matters. It was therefore ill receiced at Rome. In accordance with the usage of the Roman Courts, which are realistic in their attitudes, Newman was not judged on his intentions; certain propositions were derived from his text, and these, in isolation from their general context, had a heterodox flavor. The prejudices which until then had, so to speak, hung in the air, now took definite shape, for his critics could point in justification to a text and to "propositions" in that text. Newman became vulnerable, and he was again the suspect of a Church. From the time of publication of this article, he was, in Rome at least, under a cloud.

It was, no doubt, because of *The Rambler* article that Msgr. Talbot, who had such influence with Pius IX, wrote to Manning: "If a check be not placed on the laity of England they will be rulers of the Catholic Church in England instead of the Holy See and Episcopate." And he added what Coulson calls his "celebrated" question: "What is the province of the laity? To hunt, to shoot, to entertain. These matters they understand, but to meddle with ecclesiastical matters they have no right at all, and this affair of Newman is a matter purely ecclesiastical. . . . Dr. Newman is the most dangerous man in England, and you will see that he will make use of the laity against your Grace." (Cited by Coulson: *op. cit.*, pp. 41-42).

"To examine many photographs of Newman," writes Coulson (*op. cit.*, p. 48), "is to learn that as he grew older suffering entrenched itself upon his features." He turned into himself, devoting himself to the interior life and nourishing a yet deeper devotion to the Blessed Sacrament. He trusted in God alone and in justifying Time:

"Leaving the case to Time, who solves all doubt
By bringing Truth, her glorious daughter, out."
Newman liked to cite this couplet from Crabb.

He ceased writing, or at least publishing, until the pamphlet by Kingsley stirred him to write his *Apologia pro Vita Sua*. He himself says that *The Rambler* trouble was the reason why he wrote nothing between 1859 and 1864. It may have been that this preparatory period of silence was the source of the accumulated creative energy which went into the production of his masterpiece. It could be said that *The Rambler* affair which had caused Pius IX to distrust Newman, was also the primary cause of the reparation made by Leo XIII when he created him a Cardinal. We know that this decision of the new Pope was taken as a result of a request made by the Duke of Norfolk in the name of all the laity of England. There was a poetic relevance in this: he was reinstated at the

instance of those through whose cause he had almost come
to shipwreck.

———

Let us recall here the outline of Newman's life.

He was born in London February 21, 1801, and was
brought up in "the religion of the Bible" and in hatred of
"Popery." In 1818, we went up to Trinity College, Oxford,
and on April 12, 1822 he was elected Fellow of Oriel
College. Ordained deacon in the Anglican Church (1824),
he became a curate of St. Clement's, Oxford, until 1828,
when he became a tutor at Oriel and vicar of St. Mary's
Oxford. To re-awaken in the established Church the apostolic faith, and to withdraw it from the tutelage of the
State, he published, with some friends at Oxford, among
them Keble, Froude and Pusey, the *Tracts for the Times*.
In 1837 and 1838, he exercised great influence through
teaching, controversy, preaching, and personal ascendency.
But, after having sought to justify the Anglican Church,
in which he found a *Via Media* between Roman "corruptions" and Protestant "errors," he was led, through studying
the heresies of the fourth and fifth centuries, to revise his
system, for he saw that his *Via Media* revived the doctrines
of the Semi-Arians. He then (September 25, 1843) retired
to Littlemore, in the Oxford countryside, to subject his
doubts to the test of criticism. The history of the first six
Christian centuries led him to conclude to the substantial
identity of Roman Catholicism and of primitive Christianity, the differences being explained by the principle
of *development*. His conversion followed (October 9,
1845).

After a period in Rome, where he was ordained a
Catholic priest on May 30, 1847 (Trinity Sunday), Newman returned to England. He had decided to follow the

Rule of St. Philip Neri. With fellow converts, he established a first oratory at Maryvale (February 1, 1848). On February 10, 1852, he took up residence in the Oratory at Edgbaston, Birmingham, where he spent the rest of his life.

Despite the sympathy which high Catholic authorities ceaselessly manifested towards him, the Catholic Hierarchy of England had not yet got round to understanding or supporting him, and the consequent misunderstandings largely account for the failure of the works which Newman agreed to undertake: the Rectorship of a Catholic University in Dublin (1854-1858), the direction of an historical and critical review, *The Rambler* (1855-1859). In 1863, Newman believed himself to be abandoned by everyone, and he had doubts about his work.

However, in 1864, he was stung by Kingsley's attack into writing his *Apologia pro Vita Sua,* which won the hearts of the English public. In 1872, he published his *Grammar of Assent* to justify the logic of the act of faith. Two years later (1872) he defended against Gladstone the legitimacy of the recent definition of Papal infallibility, he himself having, prior to 1870, contested the opportuneness of such a definition. Pope Leo XIII set the seal on his work by creating him a Cardinal on May 12, 1879. He lived for ten years more, surrounded by universal veneration, and he died at Birmingham, in the midst of his brethren, on August 11, 1890. On his memorial at Edgbaston are the words: *ex umbris et imaginibus ad veritatem* and *cor ad cor loquitur.* They can be read as summing up what he himself regarded as the meaning of his life.

IDEAS

1

On Consulting the Laity

In 1848, John Moore Capes, an old friend of Newman at Oxford and like him a convert, founded a monthly with the somewhat whimsical title, *The Rambler*. The object of a Catholic review such as this was to create a body of thought against the false intellectualism of the age, to surround Catholicism with the defenses demanded for that age, to consider from the Catholic viewpoint the discoveries of that age and to give them a Catholic interpretation.

The aim of this review was, therefore, to bring together the Church and the Modern World. The collaborators were laymen, and as such they regarded themselves as independent of ecclesiastical authority when they dealt with lay subjects. They "rambled" through subjects of topical interest, dealing with problems of criticism, of history, of philosophy, exercising absolute liberty in these studies, and adopting what we should today call an attitude of commitment. One is reminded, no doubt, of the efforts made in the same direction by the liberal Catholics, Lacordaire and Montalembert.

In fact, *The Rambler* was much more scientific and

cultural than political. One of its contributors, John Acton, German on his mother's side, was a disciple of Döllinger, and his historical learning was already outstanding. *The Rambler*, whose circulation did not exceed 800, had nevertheless a major influence on the educated public.

Unhappily, this review exceeded its bounds by venturing into regions reserved to the Hierarchy. It criticised the system of education in seminaries as organized by the Council of Trent. It attacked the doctrine of eternal punishment. It called in doubt the temporal power of the Pope. Its contributors did not seek the *Imprimatur*. The attitude of *The Rambler* towards the Bishops was carping and provocative. The sympathies deliberately inclined towards the most advanced opinions. Severe in their attitude towards the Roman doctrines, the editors were highly indulgent towards the views that attacked tradition. *The Rambler* was viewed with distrust by the Bishops, even by Wiseman whose constant desire was to clear up misunderstandings between the Church and the public.

Newman was more sensitive than others to the defects of the movement, and yet he long devoted himself to combat on two fronts. He defended *The Rambler* with the Bishops and asked that it should be given its chance to prove itself. With the editors, however, he defended the Bishop's viewpoint, urging that account be taken of the remarks of the lawful authority.

At that time, he had retired from the world. Since 1858, he had resigned the rectorship of the Catholic University of Dublin, and was then living in the Oratory at Birmingham. If we are to understand properly the decision he was then to take, the way he was about to take—above parties, above even the best and most sincere minds, guided only by the duty of his own vocation—we must make our viewpoint coincide with his lofty attitude towards the historic movement of 1859 and of the London-Rome axis.

Newman who always combined studies of the Christian past with an active participation in present conflicts, saw the state of affairs in a symbolic manner.

In persons and in events, he discerned *types*; in other words, he looked beyond the persons and the events to what they signified. Hence to understand either his thoughts or his actions, a typological method must be used. We must see behind the individuals the eternal attitudes of which, for Newman, these individuals are the incarnation in the flux of time. Thus, Newman recognized himself in Athanasius, just as later on he recognized the Anglican Church in the Semi-Arians and in the Donatists. Conversely, in Lord Acton or Simpson, as in G. Ward or Dalgrain, he discerned spiritual attitudes which recur constantly in history and which are connected with the current mental attitude—an attitude always limited as regards religious truth, the latter being so difficult to grasp in its integrity.

The Rambler movement brought him face to face with an essential problem, for it was, as it were, the other side of the Oxford Tractarian movement. To sanctify the Church by bringing it back to its source, by the regeneration of the Priesthood, that was indeed the first duty. But it is the nature of a spring to overflow, to fructify the dry places, and therefore the second duty was to go out *to meet the age*. This new world called itself the Modern Age. What was necessary to this meeting was, as a friend of Newman put it, "a new philosophy, an evolved Christianity" which would restore her intellectual rights to the Church of Rome.

Now, despite defects born of exuberance, it was precisely this that the young editorial staff of *The Rambler* had attempted. In the convergence of ideas which united these young men, in spite of serious original differences, Newman could discern a reflection of the Oxford Movement. He could have said of this second "awakening" what he was saying of the first. An identical call went out simultaneously in places far removed, and it had gathered together men hitherto strangers. That is why the phenomenon in question is, in a certain sense, completely independent of visible and historical happenings. It is not in this place or in that, nor can progress, or causes, or accidents be predicted of it. It is not a movement, but a spirit which spreads itself abroad, which does not dwell in the desert nor "in the secrecy of chambers," for it is everywhere. It is within us; it awakens in our hearts when we least expect it; it makes its way, not indeed in secret, but in a manner so subtle, so impalpable, that the ordinary opposition of mankind can neither guard against nor attack it. It is an adversary dispersed, so to speak, in the air, and yet having everywhere the qualities of unity and completeness. Wherever it is, it is whole and entire; it cannot be reached or seized, for it is the result of causes far more profound than political alliances or any visible agency. It is the spiritual awakening of spiritual needs.

From this point of view, Newman excused in advance the excesses inevitable in everything that springs to life, such excesses being, as it were, shock troops with clamorous voices who act without thought or restraint. "There are always," says Newman, "souls too young to be wise, too ardent to be moderate, too intellectual to be humble" souls whose degree of sincerity one cannot assess in advance of the proof of events, and whom one does not know whether to encourage or condemn.

Newman's sympathies inclined him towards the friends of Lord Acton. He sensed vividly the darkness and the difficulties that surround the luminous point of truth. He had an intense appreciation of the evil that "a rigid and pitiless dogmatism" can create: he was aware that liberalism was no longer a party, but had become coterminous with the whole educated world.

But here again, the moment came when Newman had to break with his friends.

The articles by Lord Acton and the staff of *The Rambler*—articles sometimes rash, often paradoxical, always aggressive—did not seem to him conducive to peace, for they tended to irritate the authorities without convincing the public. It was certainly necessary to meet the new needs of thinking men, to answer their perplexities. *Illi in vos saeviant* ... said Newman, quoting St. Augustine, and he goes on to comment on the implacability of those who do not appreciate how difficult it is to discern error from truth and to discover the way of life among the illusions of this world. But at the same time Newman reproaches the editors of *The Rambler* with a failure of *timing*, since novelty is often error for minds not prepared to receive it.

Newman had never considered that religious truth dwelt in innovation, in linguistic criticism and the unravelling of enigmas. He always professed a loyal submission to religious authority. This is clear from a letter to Acton in which he criticises Simpson: "He will always be clever, amusing, brilliant, and *suggestive*. He will always be flicking his whip at Bishops, cutting them in tender places, throwing stones at Sacred Congregations, and, as he rides along the high road, discharging pea-shooters at Cardinals who happen by bad luck to look out of the window" (*Ward*: I, p. 529).

He sometimes recognized, in his "friends" of *The Rambler,* the lineaments of that intolerance to which they were exposing themselves, and even the methods of rationalism. As he points out in a letter to Lord Acton, the man who sets himself against legitimate authority is in a false position. To go against authorized authority, he says, is no proof of courage, for they have the responsibility and we should leave it to them. Such was the position of Newman towards the liberals.

Neither, however, did he approve the narrow minds of the other camp, those who would seek, he says, to transform the Faith into a system—an undertaking he regarded as both useless and hazardous. It is rash to systematize in circumstances where knowledge is limited, where the reason is active, where the established truths are very few in comparison with the wide field open to speculation. Rather should we be on our guard that our deductions do not exceed the limits of wisdom, that our conjectures do not arrogate to themselves the character of certitude. When it organizes adequate knowledge, the system is the true soul, or more precisely the philosophical formal cause; but it only creates or tends to create doctrinaires and sectaries when it attempts to organize incomplete knowledge. Yet some have undue confidence in the power of argument, so that they come to regard their opinion as the sum or the substance of the Gospel. They deliberately emphasize this or that dogma in isolation from and to the detriment of the rest. They are always ready to find clear and decisive explanations for what are really mysteries. They consider that their viewpoint is the only reasonable one. If they cite Scripture, they tell you with full assurance what each verse signifies, ought to signify, and cannot signify. They have a special vocabulary regarded as sacrosanct and, though of recent date, this vocabulary is for them as sacred as the words of Scripture or of the Church. Consequently, new terms make them dizzy, for they cannot clothe their ideas in unaccustomed garments or think of them except in their established setting. In short, they are rigid minds, and this sort of stubborn commitment proceeds from an inability to understand the relationship of the truth to its formula. Newman calls this *"bigotry."*

Such are Newman's observations on the two types of narrowness and rigidity of mind he calls *"rationalism"* and *"bigotry."*

Fundamentally, "rationalism" and "bigotry" arise from one and the same weakness. We remark in passing that, as a result of this rigidity almost congenital to the intelligence, religious truth is as easy to attack as it is difficult to defend. For what is an *objection* if not a part of truth detached from the whole, or more precisely detached from the surface of the whole? The more superficial the objection and the further removed from the core of truth, the more striking it appears. In order to attack, the freethinker has only to describe the dispersed, external and partial aspects of the truth which are exposed to his doubts. On the other hand, the would-be defender, finding himself able to produce only a fragment, attempts to gather together the dispensed lines, but the result is often an artificial process. Such are Newman's views on the behavior of the human mind.

With such a mental attitude, with such evidence of balance in the repudiation of opposed errors, Newman should have found his best friends and defenders in the Court of Rome. But, at this juncture, Newman did not find in Rome a milieu favorable to the understanding of his ideas. There the scholastic mentality prevailed; furthermore, there was the personal element of his own impressionable, sensitive, highly Anglo-Saxon nature, so little designed for disputation, so given to sufferance.

No one was more fundamentally Catholic than Newman and, in a certain sense, more a *son* and even a *father* of the Church. But his cast of mind was not Latin: he had not been formed in the habits of thought or in the conceptual language of the school prevalent in Rome and widespread throughout the Church. He loved individual cases, individual things, historic epochs, events, persons. He distrusted what he regarded as abstract. Furthermore, he suffered the isolation of genius: he was not given to nourishing himself on others, to consulting authors, to referring to authorities. Like all great artists, he created his language and his modes. He himself points out that the Holy Land, though small, has subdued the earth; that Greece, though poor, has formed the mind of the world. "Moses was alone. David too. And Paul, and Athanasius and Leo. Always, grace works with little."

All those who knew Newman, even those who loved him—as, for instance, Baron von Hügel—were hurt by this somewhat morose sensibility which often prevented him from being expansive, which gave him an appearance of remoteness, of distrust, of sublety. His adversary, Kingsley, asked: "What then is Newman trying to say?" In describing Newman's temperament, one is reminded of Fénelon.

Kingsley's question was raised even more emphatically by the theologians in Rome. It was their duty to establish what Doctor Newman was saying. He was an unusual convert: he was not following the normal way, nor was he attracted by the classical arguments. For example, it was not the stability of the Church that impressed him, but its 'evolution' on the same axis, its living identity, its *development*. The Roman theologians of the nineteenth century were not familiar with this aspect, even though the recent definition of the Immaculate Conception fundamentally presupposed a theory of "development."

To the subtle and tendentious theology of the Middle Ages, Newman preferred a more elegant and more fruitful teaching, modeled on the erudite image of Antiquity. He spoke as a psychologist; he was answered by logic. He asked that his works should be read as a whole and that they should be allowed to speak for themselves. His censors extracted propositions from them which, divorced from their contexts, called for serious reservations. Newman claimed that the misunderstandings often stemmed from verbal expressions, but it must be admitted that he rarely consented to change his wording. His shyness, his versatility, his art of balancing his assertions and shading them with the aid of history, his long Anglican past, all contributed to his isolation in the midst of his brethren. Certain theologians in Rome bracketed him with Hermes and Bautain. His act of conversion was welcomed, but the reasons he gave for it somewhat disturbed the settled modes of thought. Father Perrone, a Roman Jesuit, reflected the general attitude when he noted in his commonplace book: *Newman miscet et confundit omnia*. Msgr. Talbot, friend of Pius XI, writing to the future Cardinal Manning, could say in all seriousness: "Newman is the most dangerous man in England."

In the life of Newman, situations are often prophetic. The adumbrated conflict of tendencies was, as it were, the shadow image of the conflict of "modernism" and of "integrism," those two inverse forms of the virtual "heresy" of the twentieth century which revitalized one another as contradictories. As formerly Athanasius or Chrysostom, his models, Newman dominated the conflicts and guided the barque towards the open sea.

Consequently, it became necessary for him to take the helm of *The Rambler* which had got itself into troubled waters. To save the review, in other words to help it by controlling it, Newman—who was the natural intermediary between G. Ward and Acton—accepted in 1859 the editorship of *The Rambler*.

It was only after weeks of reflection and prayer that Newman reached this decision, for he feared that the convert Simpson, if his resignation scuttled the review (he was then at loggerheads with the Bishops over the schools question), might air the whole business and claim damages from the Bishops. Newman accepted the editorship of *The Rambler* as "a bitter penance" and at the request of Msgr. Ullathorne and of Cardinal Wiseman.

Newman then began a new series of *The Rambler*, but in a discreet way. No criticism was expressed or implied of those whose place he took and whose methods he nevertheless sought to modify.

At that time, there was conflict between the Bishops and the Catholic liberals about educational policy. Newman held that the opinion of the laity deserved at least to be taken into consideration. In the columns on contemporary events, unsigned but ascribed to Newman as editor, it was urged that lay opinion about the proposed Royal Commission on elementary education could be canvassed by the Bishops.

The recent definition of the Immaculate Conception was fresh in mind, and all were aware that Pius IX had sought the witness of the belief of the faithful in a dogma always so dear to them despite the reservations of certain great theologians such as St. Bernard and St. Thomas. Newman regarded himself as authorized to use the *a fortiori* argument. He wrote the following lines, which give no offense to any reader today:

"We do unfeignedly believe ... that their Lordships really desire to know the opinion of the laity on subjects in which the laity are especially concerned. If even in the preparation of a dogmatic definition the faithful are consulted, as lately in the instance of the Immaculate Conception, it is at least as natural to anticipate such an act of kind feeling and sympathy in great questions."

This was the spark that set everything blazing. Newman could be read by his eager critics as holding that this consultation of the laity was a right and that the laity with the successors of the Apostles made the law as if the laity were also the foundation of the Church.

In English, the general sense of the verb "to consult" is "to seek the opinion of another without obligation to accept opinion." But in Rome, *consultare* had an official, juridical and precise sense almost implying such an obligation. "To consult" was almost synonymous with "to demand a consultation"; and that verged on the idea of a law obliging the Church to consult the body of the faithful before the definition of a dogma.

In fact, Pius IX *indirectly* gathered the opinions of the laity before proclaiming the dogma of the Immaculate Conception, as did Pius XII before that of the Assumption. The opinions of the Bishops were sought about the definition and its opportuneness, and the Bishops answered, not in their own name alone, but also in the name of their diocesans, of whom the laity formed the much greater part.

To clarify his ideas, Newman wrote a long article in *The Rambler* (July 1859) entitled: "On Consulting the Faithful in Matters of Doctrine." It was reproduced in full in this book. In this introductory section, we are concerned with its immense significance in the life of Newman.

O felix culpa! This little word "consult," perhaps imprecise and certainly causing a stir, has been instrumental in giving us some admirable *retractions,* in the Augustinian sense of the word *retractatio,* where it does not signify an "amend honorable" or "withdrawal," but rather "a new study," a deeper sounding.

The phrase first disturbed Doctor Gillow, professor of theology at Ushaw. He wrote to Newman that his opinion was equivalent to placing the infallibility of the Church in the community of the faithful and not exclusively in the *Ecclesia docens.* Newman could be regarded therefore, as taking the absolutely untenable position that the fallible part of the Church could serve as guide to the infallible part. Msgr. Ullathorne pointed out that, in 1848, Pius IX had directed the Bishops to declare the attitude of their clergy. It was in an indirect and prudent fashion that he interrogated the laity, not by consulting them, but by interpreting the convictions implied in their faith, their prayer, their devotion.

Newman defended himself with little heart. Faced with the misunderstandings and especially with the shabby behavior of some, he retired into a kind of indifference. The same attitude is noticeable in Fénelon during the controversies about Quietism. Men of such noble and balanced nature, sure of their good faith, are not over-eager to explain and defend themselves against erroneous judgments, even when they are caught in a storm of criticism. As formerly during his Oxford times, when he was attacked by the mediocre, Newman sometimes used the weapon of irony, and this certainly did not pacify the administrative minds. Nevertheless, through the intermediary of Wiseman, Newman sent a defense to the Holy Office, but Wiseman neglected to deliver it. Later, Cardinal Manning was to do the same thing in very serious circumstances.

But if Newman lacked diplomacy; if, thoroughly alerted about his enemies, he was insufficiently on his guard against his friends and superiors, there was no doubt that he was perfectly clear about his own doctrine. He would not withdraw until he had proof. He maintained his right, even his duty, to write in the common language when he addressed himself to the laity. He had used the verb *to consult* in the sense sanctioned by usage and by the dictionary.

In *The Rambler* article, Newman said that there had been a temporary "suspense" of the function of the teaching Church during a certain period of the fourth century. Newman explained that by "suspense" he meant "suspension." *Suspension* implies indecision and not absence; the latter idea would be implicit had he used the word *failure*. He had said that *the body of the laity*, had been faithful, while *the body of the Bishops* had not been so. In a letter of September 2, he explained to his principal critic, Doctor Gillow, that by the body of the Bishops he meant the actual assembly of Bishops at that time, and nothing more. Nor by the term "general council" did he mean an ecumenical council, but simply a council assembling all the Bishops of a region. It is true that, even in the case of a great writer, ordinary language lacks the precision of technical language. It is a difficult task to make oneself clearly understood at once by the London laity and by the Roman theologians.

But underneath these academic disputes over verbal niceties, there was, as Doctor Gillow rightly stressed, a problem of principle. Newman made his position clear, and did not retreat from it.

His idea, which became more precise with time and

with study, never varied essentially. It consisted in making
a distinction between the unanimous faith of the Church,
which belongs to it as a community, and the power of
defining that faith, which power is the province of the
Hierarchy and of the teaching Church.

In practice, when the Church defines its faith while
evoking the witness of Tradition, it does not confine itself
to assembling the declarations of the Holy See and the
councils of Bishops. It also gathers together the prayers,
the liturgies, the customs; it seeks to determine the
general assent of the faithful—an assent which is, as it
were, an unsophisticated wisdom, a global intuition, *a
phronèsis,* an instinct for truth, an inspiration of the Holy
Spirit which often manifests itself in the laity by a spontaneous horror of error.

This being understood, it is for the teaching Church
to control, if necessary to authenticate, this instinct, dis-
engaging it from its imperfect expressions and giving it
a valid and precise theological meaning. The teaching
Church as such is infallible; in their capacity of private
persons, the Pope, the Bishops, the theologians can be
fallible.

Newman added a third theme especially connected
with his particular studies of the fourth century. In at
least one set of circumstances, it would have been difficult
to preserve *the deposit of faith* if account had not been
taken of the witness of the laity. In the course of history,
it is true, some of the laity followed the innovators, but
it is also true that the faith of the laity was more loyal
than that of a part of the Clergy or of certain very outstanding theologians.

The position is clear: while the *definition* of the Faith
has been confided to the successors of the Apostles *in union
with* the successor of St. Peter, or to the Pope speaking in

their name, the *development* of revelation has been confided to all those who have been baptized in Jesus Christ.
Christ, for Newman, is an individual Person Whose likeness has been implanted in the mind and heart of all the
faithful—laity, Bishops, Priests. It is this holy community
that is the whole Church, and the Church continually
develops in knowledge and in love.

2

The Triple Office of the Laity

This idea of "consulting" the laity, which Newman had used almost incidentally in his Rambler editorial, was deeper in him than perhaps he himself realized.

The doctrine of the Anglican Church had, as we know, a twofold source: the Church of the first Christian centuries, and the doctrines of Luther and Calvin.

The first of these sources led Newman to contemplate this early period of the Catholic Church. From the very beginning, the sacramental distinction existed between the laity and the priests, but there was less obvious distinction than now prevails between the "lay" element and the "pastoral" element of the Church. This can be accounted for by the spirit of community characteristic of the Eastern Christian, or by the influence of Greek philosophy emanating from Alexandria, or the conditions in Rome where the Christians, faced with persecution, went into hiding and became united in one and the same flock gathered around the first Popes. It was after the conversion of Constantine that the state hierarchy (in which the distinction between the sacred and the lay was so pronounced) imprinted its likeness on the ecclesiastical state and helped to separate it from the lay world, while souls seeking sanctity were leaving this confused world for the silence of the deserts.

The other source, the Lutheran, emphatically upheld the liberty of the Christian. It accented the call of the Christian vocation which constituted the man of faith: the monk, the priest, was no longer a privileged person. Utterly dissimilar sources created an ambivalence in Anglicanism. But each nourished the other. The mixture of authenticity and protest gave an obscure, ill-defined, sometimes repressed, but powerful strength to the claims of the laity.

On the other hand, since lay value and importance was, like other elements, monopolized by heresy, Rome accentuated yet more her suspicion of lay initiative. In another work (*Le Christ écartelé*) I have shown that this suspicion had its roots in the Donatist crisis, when the course which lay prophetism could take became clear—that religion of the Spirit which the lay element sometimes tends to inaugurate, dissolving the principle of ecclesiastical institution.

The Reformation had undermined the Catholic idea of the Priesthood, and had made all the laity potential priests. It was only to be expected that the Counter-Reformation should have regarded with suspicion any doctrine of practice which tended to give to laymen rights or powers assimilable to those of Bishops and Priests. The gap which, by the Middle Ages, divided the clergy from the laity, because of the hierarchical structure of the Church and because of the feudal structure of society, became an abyss at the time of the Reformation. An attempt to fill in that abyss has begun only in our times with the Second Vatican Council.

Newman's idea about the place of the laity in the Church stems from his whole doctrine, from his whole action, from his whole system of thought.

If we would find the first source, we must undoubtedly seek it, as is always the case with Newman, in a religious experience, or more precisely in an experience resulting from a Gospel meditation. I am inclined to believe that the mystical origin of Newman's reflections on the laity is the *logion,* gathered by the most ancient oral tradition, on the place of the prophet John the Baptist in the kingdom of heaven. John is the greatest prophet of the Old Testament, and yet Jesus declares that the least in the kingdom of heaven is greater than John. Newman's characteristic reflection on this *logion* is that the humble stones of the eternal evangelical pavement are of greater value than the cornerstone of the Temple of Israel.

Newman is here thinking of that mystical reality which the First Epistle of St. Peter calls the house of the Spirit, a holy priesthood, living stones. And this temple made with living stones, which is the spiritual Jerusalem, seems to him to surpass in splendor that of Solomon in all his glory. "The hidden saints are enough to carry out God's noiseless work," says Newman later on. It may be that at this juncture of his Anglican life, the cornerstone of the ancient Temple represented the established priesthood, such as he saw it in this slumbering Church which he sought *to awaken.*

Newman went almost to excessive lengths when he celebrated (February 22, 1835), in accents at once Biblical and romantic, the role of intercession played by each Christian who develops the seed of Baptism and Confirmation: "... standing in God's presence upright and irreprovable, accepted in the Beloved, clad in the garments of righteousness, anointed with oil, and with a crown on his head, in royal and priestly garb, as an heir of eternity, full of grace and good works, as walking in all the commandments of the Lord blameless, such an one, I repeat it, is plainly in his fitting place where he intercedes." (*Parochial and Plain Sermons*, III. pp. 362-363).

Such is the first *vision* of the laity according to Newman; in it he concentrates the teachings of the Old Testament about the prophet. Newman discerned that the laity of the Christian world are in the current of prophetism.

In a sermon preached in the Church of St. Mary at Oxford, he develops this mystical ideal, pregnant but still obscure, by applying to it the classic distinction of the three *offices* of Christ.

The faithful, he says, reproduce Christ. They too are, therefore, in a way he goes on to define, *kings, priests, prophets*.

How are they kings? What privilege of a royal kind would Newman confer on the laity? Where is to be found the new equivalent of the unction which creates the king? Newman teaches that the layman is a king when he works and when he endures, for work is the Christian mode of true royalty, of the real possession and domination of the earth. Perhaps he is here thinking of the mysterious promise of the Beatitudes: "Blessed are the meek for they shall possess the land."

How can the layman share in the priesthood, since he has neither the function nor the power? He is a priest, Newman answers, in as much as he is called to practice prayer and endurance.

Thus the layman is "king" through work, "priest" through suffering, "doctor" through witness of the teaching and teaching of the witness.

"Christ came to make a new world," says Newman.

"He came into the world to regenerate it in Himself, to make a new beginning, to be the beginning of the creation of God, to gather together in one and recapitulate all things in Himself. The rays of His glory were scattered through the world; one state of life had some of them, another others. The world was like some fair mirror, broken in pieces, and giving back no one uniform image of its Maker. But He came to combine what was dissipated, to recast what was shattered, in Himself."

This is the Biblical and mystical humus whence Newman derived his ideas about the laity. One can sense the commentary he could have made on that famous text about the "priesthood" of the laity in the First Epistle of Peter, where the spirit of the Old Testament is sublimated in the New Order.

Newman's intuition about the laity is concentrated in his Rambler article and especially in that word "consulting" which is like the tiny drop of water which reflects a sky of stars. I see Newman's thought as a reversed cone whose base extends itself indefinitely, but whose apex, a very delicate point, concentrating in itself the entire mass, is expressed by the short phrase "consulting the faithful." What we write almost in passing, often recapitulates ourselves.

———

Newman's thought oscillates between two poles. The first is a *logic of assent;* the second is *an ontology of development.*

In the first, Newman attacks the important problem of justifying the faith of the unlearned man, of showing how such a man believes in a reasonable fashion without however being able to justify, logically and theologically, the distinct reasons for his faith, since such reasons are based on a metaphysic and a history of which he knows very little. To do this, Newman is obliged to explore those ways of the human reason of which the reason knows nothing because they exist a little below the level of consciousness.

But it was necessary that he should also quit the domain of nature and of history—where we have only experiences which are indirect, onerous and inaccessible to the majority of men—for the domain of morality.

Newman then distinguishes between *inference* and *assent*. Inference is always incomplete, indirect, inadequate, and ultimately rests on probabilities; assent is absolute. However, we possess "an illative sense" which enables us to realize the intimate accord of thought and being in which the Greeks recognized the mark of certitude. This communion exists where the ancients did not think of seeking it—in the moral conscience. The conformity of the moral order with the light of Revelation is felt in a confused manner by the man of good will, whence his assurance in believing what is not clearly seen. More than Descartes, Newman knew that the act by which one believes something, is different from that by which one knows that one believes it. If we are to judge a man, we must discount what he says (for this is often a logical invention designed to disguise his feelings), in order to concentrate our attention on his actions and on the beliefs which these actions reveal.

But this latent faith which cannot justify itself and which in a sense Newman prefers because it is a lived faith, is it not the faith of the little ones, of the laity? It is the faith of the *people;* it is the faith of an educated laity not versed in theology.

Now, the thought of the people and that of the élite follow analogous ways. For both, the work of reason consists in enabling a seed to mature which exists already from the beginning. The savant must undergo the proof of "the explicit reason," with its many attendant perils; while the practice of duty enables the average man, basing himself on the accord of his moral experiences, to give a correct assent to the truths of faith.

That is why it is good *to consult* this Christian who, though at first sight incompetent, has greater implicit richness than he realizes.

When he was still an Anglican, Newman's attention was caught by the popular devotions held in honor of Catholicism. His difficulty was to discern, by solid criteria, what in Roman teaching is revealed doctrine and what is only opinion, tolerated piety, and ultimately pious legend. As an Anglican, he sought to follow a middle way between the excesses of Protestantism which suppressed everything, and the excesses of Roman Catholicism which accepts nearly everything in the traditions. For one could not, in the Protestant manner, limit faith to the Scriptures, but neither could one extend it, as did the Catholics, to all the corruptions of devotion.

Newman was therefore led to distinguish two traditions. One is fixed in the Baptismal Symbol and is transmitted from Bishop to Bishop and set before the eyes of every Christian. Furthermore, this tradition is not limited to those very concise documents known as Creeds; it is also expressed in rites and ceremonies, which are much more than pure oral traditions and which witness to belief in the objects of which they are the signs. All this constitutes "the episcopal tradition"; it is the "hypotyposis" about which St. Paul speaks to Timothy.

But side by side with this tradition, Newman places what he calls "the prophetic tradition." St. Paul, he says, regarded the prophets and doctors as the interpreters of

Revelation. They develop it and define its mysteries, they clarify its documents, they harmonize its content, they apply its promises. Their teaching is a vast system which cannot be expressed in a few phrases or summed up in a single code or treatise. It is a certain body of truths which is diffused through the Church like an atmosphere, and which is irregular because of its profusion. At certain epochs this tradition coincides with the episcopal tradition; at other times, it dissolves in fables and legends. It is partly written, partly oral, partly the supplement of Scripture; now conserved in intellectual expression, now hidden in the mind and the temperament of Christians. Here and there it is expressed in liturgies, in works of controversy, in obscure fragments, in popular prejudices, in local customs. The prophetic tradition is what St. Paul calls *tò-phrónema tou pneúmatos* (Rom., VIII, 6), the thought of the Spirit, the character, the temperament, the breath of the Church. Or better still, it is the Church in action as distinct from the Church quiescent.

But the prophetic tradition is indefinable, since it is lived rather than formulated. It is especially subject to corruption, if the Church is not vigilant. On the other hand, who can draw the boundary line between the episcopal tradition and the prophetic tradition, between what must be believed and what it is perhaps better to believe than to reject, between the essential and the non-essential, between the domain of faith and that of "devotion"? Doctrine defines belief once and for all, and is therefore incapable of growth, whereas devotion does mature; it colors belief and it can degenerate into serious errors.

———

Let us now consider the idea of *development*. It presents two aspects. The first is well known: the identity of revealed truth, once it has been cast into the flux of time, must grow in forms and in formulas, must become more explicit, must change according to appearance. Development (this *way* of identity at work in time) reconciles *truth* and *life*, a highly improbable accord which is found only in the Roman Catholic axis, where it finds its guarantee in the existence of an infallible authority.

Thus, as I have already pointed out, besides the physical and mathematical identity (a narrow, absolute, formal identity which would fashion everything in the same mould and which nature abhors, as she abhors a vacuum), Newman pointed to an identity of life and of movement which ensures the permanence of the idea by the equivalence of its successive manifestations. As distinct from the borrowed and tainted life which maintains itself by artifices, Newman sang the praises of the true life which conserves itself by renewing itself, whose recessions are temporary, whose very dust is spiritual, and which by its existential energy multiplies on all sides its likenesses, manifesting itself whole and entire in the smallest morsels of the body which it animates. Newman suggests that, besides the "evolution" of material things which is simply a metamorphosis, there could be an intimate change proper to spiritual beings. This is *development*.

But here again, the work of the faithful is placed in a new light. Faith is no longer seen as a static gift, as a closed treasure which could be labelled once for all; it lives in the whole body of believers who, throughout time, labor, to make it explicit. Hence, the faith is not the special possession of an élite or of a sacerdotal body, however perfect, who alone would have the keys of the sanctuary of truth; it is shared by all the members of the Church. And each, according to his place, his experience and his lights, is called upon to contribute to the fructification of this faith by works and by knowledge. The laity have not received the charge *to define*, that is to *decide magisterially* about matters under discussion. For this, an authority is required, and even, said Newman at the end of his Anglican period, a definitive authority provided with a charisma which preserves it from error. But the laity is the living part of the Tradition at work. It is through the laity that this tradition becomes explicit, as emerges when we study the history of dogmas, and especially, as has often been noted, the history of what has been defined by the Church concerning the privileges of Mary, the Mother of God.

"And Mary kept all these things in her heart." Newman, who loved this text, has applied it to the whole Church, of which the Blessed Virgin is the figure and the recapitulation. For Newman, she was also the image of this development of faith by reflection and love, by work and by sacrifice, by the oblation of the whole of life in all its aspects. Is it possible that he saw in her, perhaps, the archetype of the laity?

He was always emphatic that the Holy Spirit works in the Church in ways of simplicity, of seeming naivety, of divine candor, in short through some mysterious "instinct" of common piety, especially at times when theologians, following their straight road of logic, end in erroneous or abstract positions. The laity, as well as the Hierarchy, share in their own way in the offices of Jesus Christ, by promoting the kingdom of God through their works and by offering themselves in their sufferings that Christ's kingdom may "come."

The Holy Spirit guides the Church by the order of government and by the order of witness. Now, in this second domain, the laity have a very living part. Both as a body and as individuals, the laity must bear witness.

Whether they help the apostles to teach the nations, or whether they labor to make the Church more conscious of the deposit of faith, the laity, in union with the Hierarchy, are witnesses to and shapers of their Faith.

As Father Davis of Birmingham University, one of the greatest authorities on Newman, has pointed out, all the faithful, and not solely the theologians, have their role to play in the development of doctrine. The Word of God has come down on earth in the human form of Christ, as well as through the words of Scripture. The knowledge of that Word was transmitted to Christians in the mode of a personal knowledge. As Newman has reminded us in his "Grammar of Assent," Christ is One whose likeness has been implanted in the minds and hearts of millions. He is a Person whom they know and love. In contemplation and in prayer, they learn to know Him better. But this is something rarely achieved by mere reasoning about Him. It is probable that Newman was led to this conclusion by a tendency he invariably showed to defend the average man against the specialists. His "Grammar of Assent" was written to prove that ordinary men and women, without particular qualifications in theology or philosophy, can discover a way to the faith—a way which, while not formal or syllogistic, is truly reasonable. Similarly, his "Essay on the Development of Dogma" is an attempt to show how, when the Holy Spirit dwells in a body of the faithful such as the Christian Church, that body will inevitably increase its grasp of the Faith. This occurs through a living growth of the intelligence, the result of long familiarity with Christ. Father Davis goes on to say that, more accurately, this occurs, not so much by any efforts of the faithful to reason their way to Christ, as by the fact that Christ exercises an increasingly profound influence on their spirit. It is much more, he says, that Christ takes possession of

Christians than that they take possession of Christ. (Colloque de Strasbourg, 1959).

Thus, *assent* and *development*, concepts typical of Newman, cast a twofold light on the meaning of the verb *to consult*.

3

Arianism and the Laity

Newman was one of those who foresee before they act how that action will appear to them afterwards. Like Plato, like Goethe, like Pater, Proust or Du Bos, he had the impression of simply remembering what he was really discovering. Hence the study in depth of certain episodes of past history was necessary to his perception of present events. He found history indispensable to his understanding of what was occurring here and now.

For him, as for the prophets of Israel, the future was prefigured in the past. By studying certain significant periods of the past, he sought the shape of things to come. In his view, the whole history of the Church was, for the Church, a simple, mysterious, adumbrating and reassuring typology, as the Old Testament had been for the early Christians: it presented signs, notifications, prefigurations, as though what was at present obscurely happening had occurred already. There were, for instance, in the early centuries, the conduct of the Church, its discipline, the sentiments it inspired—curiosity, distrust, calumny, revulsion; in the fourth century, its often considerable failures;

its organization, its power, its Catholicity, the divisions and cartels of its enemies who were often ready to shelve their own differences to unite against the Church; the schisms and the caesaropapism which was on the alert for them; the heresies—their hatreds, their excesses, their wide circulation, their fortunes, their varieties and their variations; in the fifth and sixth centuries, the intimate life of the Church—its weaknesses, its negligences, and, amid so many disorders and subjects for fear, the permanence of Roman fidelity. All these distinct traits, united but permanent, helped Newman to understand the Church of the twentieth century. It was a tacit axiom of his Catholic philosophy that the Roman Church conforms at each epoch to its Type: it constantly and cumulatively bears the likeness of its whole past, for the Eternal is in time.

This habit of seeing the past of the present in the present of the past was already his when, in his early years, Hugh James Rose (who, with Lyall, was editing a theological library) asked him to write a history of the first Councils. Newman saw in this request the "call" he needed to begin his work.

At first, he limited himself to the Council of Nicaea, but he was inevitably drawn also to the study of the pre-history of that Council and especially to the study of the Church of Alexandria. The result was his book, "The Arians of the Fourth Century"—the labor of whose composition remained vividly with him into old age. Looking back on it, he criticized it severely as the work of a single year, inexact in thought, incorrect in language. This, at the time, was not the opinion of H. J. Rose, who was greatly excited by certain parts of the manuscript; nor was it the opinion of Döllinger who, in 1857, wrote to Newman that his "Arians" would be read by future generations as a model of its kind. When Newman was working on the "Remains" of Froude, he remarked in a letter to Rogers that we never have the history of men in the most interesting period of their lives, from eighteen to twenty-eight or thirty, when they are in process of formation. His "Arians" and the two-volumed "Annotated Translation of Athanasius" were the fruits of those first years of apprenticeship. There one already finds the usual methods of Newman, a first sketch of his theology and his logic, and the silhouettes of that early Church which he loved so well. It is by no means fanciful to find in them, with all their original savor, the ideas that were to give to his mature works their unity and their value.

On Newman's study of the origins and consequences of the Council of Nicaea, he uncovers the efforts of the laity, in the defense of the faith. He considered that, without the laity, at a certain point in the fouth century, the faith of that Council would have been compromised.

———

In "The Arians," Newman poses the problem, for him a fundamental one, of the "dogmatic definition" of the faith. How did the religion of Jesus become a theological religion expressed in propositions, dogmas, anathemas? Or again, why were abstract words and formulas added to the concrete and divine language of the Scriptures? Newman was concerned with the three problems: *Why* dogma? *How* did the Council come about? *In what sense* did the faithful, the laity, participate in this elaboration of the faith?

It is difficult for us, says Newman, to put ourselves in the place of the early laity. "The idea of disbelieving or criticizing the great doctrines of the faith," he writes, "from the nature of the case would scarcely occur to the primitive Christians. These doctrines were the subject of an Apostolic Tradition; they were the very truths which had been lately revealed to mankind.... They were facts, not opinions. To come to the Church was all one with expressing a readiness to receive her teaching; to hesitate to believe, after coming for the sake of believing, would be an inconsistency too rare to require a special provision against the chance of it. It was sufficient to meet the evil as it arose: the power of excommunication and deposition was in the hands of the ecclesiastical authorities, and, as in the case of Paulus, was used impartially." (*Arians*, p. 134). Thus the ante-Nicene heresies originated with those who had never belonged to the Church or who had been expelled from it. Furthermore, the creeds which contained the Apostolic Tradition and which alone made possible the interpretation of "the obscurities of Scripture," were reserved to those already Christians or about to become Christians. These formal expressions of faith were, therefore, "withdrawn from public view"; and, without them, "Scripture . . . was scarcely more than a sealed book."

It must be added that, in Newman's view of the ante-Nicene Church, "the knowledge of the Christian mysteries was, in those times, accounted as a privilege, to be eagerly coveted." There was a reluctance to open them to "the inquirers and half-Christians," to the ignorant, to the persecutors. "If the early Church," he wrote (*Arians*, p. 136) "regarded the very knowledge of the truth as a fearful privilege, much more did she regard that truth itself as glorious and awful; and scarcely conversing about it to her children, shrank from the impiety of subjecting it to the hard gaze of the multitude." Newman was no lover of sudden and brutal enlightenment: he considered that religious truth can be attained "only by the sober and watchful, by slow degrees, with dependence on the Giver

of wisdom, and with strict obedience to the light which
has already been granted." In this connection, he remarks
on the inconvenience of the written formulas, on "the
unfitness of books, compared with private communication,
for the purpose of religious instruction; levelling, as they
do, the distinctions of mind and temper by the formality
of the written character, and conveying each kind of
knowledge the less perfectly, in proportion as it is of a
moral nature and requires to be treated with delicacy and
discrimination." In the first period of the Church's history,
each truth was taught by "private communication," with
"delicacy and discrimination," and at the proper time;
it was communicated to those who were truly ready to
profit from it, having passed through all the successive
degrees of obedience and of faith. This is what is suggested
by the "Epistle to the Hebrews and by the practice followed in the catechetical school of he Church of Alexandria. By this wisely progressive method, precaution was
taken against those who like to rush into things and sweep
aside established procedure—against what Newman calls
"a scrutinizing infidelity (which) wounds and lacerates."
How can the Gospel be explained to men until they have
been taught to know themselves, to discern the sanctity
of God, through the preparatory discipline of natural law
and of natural religion?

Heretics, on the contrary, scarcely observe this discre-
tion when they propagate their beliefs. "Arius," says Newman, "began by throwing out his questions as a subject of
debate for public consideration; and at once formed
crowds of controversialists from those classes who were
the least qualified or deserving to take part in this discussion. Thus the sacred, reserved, somewhat secret character of her doctrine left the Church defenceless . . . when
the attack of Arianism was made against it; insulting its

silence, provoking it to argue, unsettling and seducing its members, and in consequence requiring its authoritative judgment on the point in dispute" (*Arians*, p. 141). The Nicene Fathers were forced to bear witness to the truth by publicly formulating the Creed.

———

But this *exterior* call was not the only one. There was also an *interior* call proceeding from the very nature of the human mind, among both the faithful and the Clergy.

"Before the mind has been roused to reflection and inquisitiveness about its own acts and impressions," writes Newman (*Arians*, pp. 143-145), "it acquiesces, if religiously trained, in that practical devotion to the Blessed Trinity, and implicit acknowledgment of the divinity of Son and Spirit, which holy Scripture at once teaches and exemplifies. This is the faith of uneducated man, which is not the less philosophically correct, nor less acceptable to God, because it does not happen to be conceived in those precise statements which presuppose the action of the mind on its own sentiments and notions.... As the mind is cultivated and expanded, however, it cannot refrain from the attempt to analyze the vision which influences the heart, and the Object in which that vision centres, nor does it stop till it has, in some sort, succeeded in expressing in words, what has all along been a principle both of its affections and of its obedience. But ... the Object of religious veneration being unseen, and dissimilar from all that is seen, reason can but represent it in the medium of those ideas which the experience of life affords.... Thus the systematic doctrine of the Trinity may be considered as the shadow, projected from the contemplation of the intellect, of scripturally-informed piety; a representation, economical; necessarily imperfect, as being exhibited in a foreign medium, and therefore involving apparent inconsistencies or mysteries; given to the Church contemporaneously with those apostolic writings, which are addressed more directly to the heart; kept in the background in the infancy of Christianity, when faith and obedience were vigorous, and brought forward at a time when, reason being disproportionately developed, and aiming at sovereignty in the province of religion, its presence became necessary to expel an usurping idol from the house of God." This mental representation is "substantially correct," however "ineffectual all attempts ever will be to secure the doctrine by mere general language": it excludes error, it assists worship, it regulates and stimulates the Christian mind. If religious ideas are not correctly applied, "they react upon the affections, and deprave the religious principle. This is exemplified in the case of the heathen, who, trying to make their instinctive notion of the Deity an object of reflection, pictured to themselves false images, which eventually gave them a pattern and a sanction for sinning."

In these perspectives, the role of the laity appeared in a new light. To understand this role, we must recall what was at issue in the period following the Council of Nicaea.

The word *consubstantial*, introduced into the Nicene Creed, clearly and incontrovertibly excluded the error of Arius. It thus *defined* the faith. And one may ask, with Karl Barth, whether indeed (despite the inadequacy arising from the ambiguous nature of all human language) this is not the most exact word to signify what was intended. "Co-eternal," "equal," "one-with" would have been accepted by the Arians. They would not accept "consubstantial."

The history of Arianism is one of the strangest episodes in Church History. The Council of Nicaea was very soon called in question. Its adversaries did not triumph.

Arius was a man sure of himself, clever, with powerful protectors at the Imperial court. Moreover, he had the support of the Erasmus of his time, the father of ecclesiastical history, Eusebius of Caesarea, the great savant and yet, as Newman points out, a man "careless of the cause of truth . . . in comparison of the comforts and decencies of literary ease." He was under the impression that the Council of Nicea had been victorious through surprise moves and shock tactics.

Eustathius of Antioch, a Nicene theologian, kept little restraint on his tongue: he liked to recall that the Empress mother had formerly been a maidservant in an inn. Constantine exiled him to Thrace, and the see of Antioch went to a friend of Arius. Thus began those changes of incumbents which took on a great political importance. Arius had his adversaries removed. He was reinstated in the Church, and was on the point of triumphing, even at Constantinople, when he died suddenly (336). Constantine died the following year, having been baptized on his deathbed. So it came about that, in 350, one of Constantine's sons, Constantius, became sole Emperor. He favored Eusebius of Nicomedia and Eudoxius of Constantinople who sought to make Arianism the official doctrine, just as Constantine had done for the Catholicism of Nicaea and by the same methods—the calling of ecumenical councils and the stamp of formulas of belief.

It was impossible, of course, to act directly against the Council of Nicaea and against the canonical term, *consubstantial*. But the adherents of Nicaea could be removed from their episcopal sees. The great upholder of Nicaea, Athanasius, Bishop of Alexandria, was exiled. The Council,

held at Sardica, then at Sirmium, drew up professions of
faith in which the word *consubstantial* was omitted or
replaced by expressions which, although similar in kind to
those of Nicaea, could be subscribed to by the opponents
of the Nicene Faith. The most celebrated of these formulas
added an *iota* to the word *homoousios* (consubstantial),
thus obtaining the word *Homoiousios* which means "of
like substance." Clearly, this little *iota*, masquerading as
an insignificant change, destroyed everything which the
Fathers of Nicaea had sought to establish.

Violence came to the help of subtlety. In 359, a Council
was held at Rimini with four hundred Western Bishops
present, another at Seleucia in Asia Minor with one hundred and fifty Eastern Bishops, and the word *consubstantial* was rejected. It was then that St. Jerome wrote:
Ingemuit totus orbis et arianum se esse miratus est (Adv.
Lucif., 10). The major episcopal sees were in the hands
of the Semi-Arians: Lisbon, Arles, Ravenna, Sirmium in
the West; Alexandria, Jerusalem, Caesarea, Antioch, Nicomedia, Constantinople in the East. At Rome, Pope Liberius was exiled. Liberius, through an excessive spirit of
conciliation, sacrificed the principal upholder of Nicaea,
the indomitable Athanasius.

One might then suppose that the Church was about
to become Semi-Arian, that is, anti-Nicene, condemning
itself, and implicitly condemning the Papal legates who
had proposed the doctrine of consubstantiality at Nicaea.
Arian the Church then seemed in power and in appearance, but the faith of Nicaea, though silenced, had not
been extinguished. In this, Athanasius played a major part.
He was in himself, as it were, a whole Church, and the
people recognized in him a good Christian and a true
Bishop. He never gave in. Faced with the apparent success of principalities and of specious unanimities, with the

apparent "dialectic of history," he remained loyal to the truth. And thus he secured the future by fidelity to the past.

———

But Athanasius, according to Newman, had need of two-fold assistance: the Papacy and the laity.

It was a matter for wonder to Newman how many high placed Bishops there were who could not discern what was at stake, whereas the laity sensed it. He concluded that the laity should not be overlooked in the very matters which concern the faith. In spite of the extreme compromise by Pope Liberius, the Nicene faith was saved by the convergence of the faith of the people with that of a few Bishops.

From that time onwards, the idea of a *superman* to come, who would crown the efforts of humanity—an idea latent in the Western mind—could not appear in the Church. Christ alone holds such a position: superhumanity is a divine superhumanity.

This whole episode is a test case. It shows what could not fail to happen to the religion of the Incarnation if a choice had to be made between the pure mystery and the mystery reduced to more human proportions. Renan remarked that Arianism "which had the rare merit of having converted the Germans before their entry into Europe, would probably have given the world a Christianity capable of becoming rational." He meant by this, a Christianity deprived of the truly supernatural.

The laity, who were neither theologians nor politicians, who truly constituted the faithful people (the *laos* in the sense of the First Epistle of St. Peter), had the innate feeling that anything which diminished, even indirectly, the Christ God, threatened the faith which they had received. They did not enter into the subtleties of the Semi-Arian disputes, but their religious instinct guided them. Christ could not be a cosmic Christ, a supercreature. And, at the very time when the conscience of the laity refused to diminish Christ to the highest of creatures, the Christian people were preserving the idea that there was nevertheless a creature eminent among creatures, who in a sense answered to the Arian ideal—the Blessed Virgin, the "Mother of God," whom the laity of Ephesus were to acclaim.

If the faith of the laity has had such a determining effect in the development of Marian thought (as emerged in the nineteenth and twentieth centuries at the definition of the Immaculate Conception and of the Assumption), the reason is that the laity, the people, were immune from those causes of error which a specialization, a function, a perspective, and the need to distinguish oneself, ultimately entail in a doctrine. Lay instinct is, of course, prone to several deviations, the principal being popular superstition. This is the reverse side of the coin. Every gift must be paid for. As Newman has noted, while tyranny threatens the necessary office of power, while subtlety and the spirit of system menace ideas, the religious sense of the people is threatened by pagan debasement, by ritual formalism, by the symbiosis of faith and of the possession of the goods of the earth. In spite of this, it is in the depths of the people that saints are recruited. The same occurs in the natural order: from the people come the élite. Good sense, in the full original sense of the term, is the real name for complete genius, so rare among men who act and who think. Good sense in religious matters is found in its fullness only with the saints. Common sense in the original sense of its term, stands over against good sense; for common sense is merely the mediocre image of good sense, a substitute and a superstition. To return to that sad period of history which made St. Jerome tremble and which took Newman by surprise—that period in which the Church unwittingly seemed to run the risk of becoming Arian (that is, of losing the full sense of the full Mystery), it is not to be wondered at that it was the people who remained absolutely faithful. More intimately than the learned, the people had sensed that the basis of the Gospel is the mystery of God made man.

TEXTS

4

"The Rambler" Text: 1859

The accumulation and convergence of the living texts given by Newman in his article: *On Consulting the Faithful in Matters of Doctrine,* the original version of which we reproduce in this chapter, show clearly how Newman can breathe a palpitating life in his presentation of the past. Placed side by side with a great dialectical skill which only the erudite can fully appreciate, the documents speak for themselves. Yet erudition is here enlivened by poetry, and the whole is animated by that natural eloquence which Newman could call upon when stung into self-defense. Although this article marks the beginning of a six years silence, it can be regarded as the first indication of what Newman could do in defense of the right and the just. In this he is like St. Paul: *Factus sum insipiens, vos me coegistis!* After that silence, he was to produce his mighty *Apologia pro vita sua* (1864), which was to win for him the sympathy of his own people and lead to his finest hour under Leo XIII.

On Consulting the Faithful in Matters of Doctrine

A question has arisen among persons of theological knowledge and fair and candid minds, about the wording and the sense of a passage in the *Rambler* for May. It admits to my own mind of so clear and satisfactory an explanation, that I should think it unnecessary to intrude myself, an anonymous person, between the conductors and readers of this magazine, except that, as in dogmatic works the replies made to objections often contain the richest matter, so here too, plain remarks on a plain subject may open to the minds of others profitable thoughts, which are more due to their own superior intelligence than to the very words of the writer.

The *Rambler,* then, has these words at p. 122: "In the preparation of a dogmatic definition, the faithful are consulted, as lately in the instance of the Immaculate Conception." Now two questions bearing upon doctrine have been raised on this sentence, putting aside the question of fact as regards the particular instance cited, which must follow the decision on the doctrinal questions: viz. first, whether it can, with doctrinal correctness, be said that an *appeal* to the faithful is one of the preliminaries of a definition of doctrine; and secondly, granting that the faithful are taken into account, still, whether they can correctly be said to be *consulted.* I shall remark on both these points, and I shall begin with the second.

1

Now doubtless, if a divine were expressing himself formally, and in Latin, he would not commonly speak of the laity being "consulted" among the preliminaries of a dogmatic definition, because the technical, or even scientific, meaning of the word "consult" is to "consult *with*," or to

"take *counsel*." But the English word "consult," in its popular and ordinary use, is not so precise and narrow in its
meaning; it is doubtless a word expressive of trust and
deference, but not of submission. It includes the idea of
inquiring into a matter of *fact*, as well as asking a judgment.
Thus we talk of "consulting our barometer" about the
weather:—the barometer only attests the *fact* of the state
of the atmosphere. In like manner, we may consult a watch
or a sun-dial about the time of day. A physician consults
the pulse of his patient; but not in the same sense in which
his patient consults *him*. It is but an index of the state of
his health. Ecclesiastes says, "Qui *observat* ventum, non
seminat"; we might translate it, "he who consults," without
meaning that we ask the wind's opinion. This being considered, it was, I conceive, quite allowable for a writer, who
was not teaching or treating theology, but, as it were,
conversing, to say, as in the passage in question, "In the
preparation of a dogmatic definition, the faithful are consulted." Doubtless their advice, their opinion, their judgment on the question of definition is not asked; but the
matter of fact, viz. their belief, *is* sought for, as a testimony to that apostolical tradition, on which alone any
doctrine whatsoever can be defined. In like manner, we
may "consult" the liturgies or the rites of the Church; not
that they speak, not that can take any part whatever in the
definition, for they are documents or customs; but they are
witnesses to the antiquity or universality of the doctrines
which they contain, and about which they are "consulted."
And, in like manner, I cetainly understood the writer in
the *Rambler* to mean (and I think any lay reader might so
understand him) that the *fidelium sensus* and *consensus* is
a branch of evidence which it is natural or necessary for
the Church to regard and consult, before she proceeds to
any definition, from its intrinsic cogency; and by conse-

quence, that it ever has been so regarded and consulted. And the writer's use of the word "opinion" in the foregoing sentence, and his omission of it in the sentence in question, seemed to show that, though the two cases put therein were analogous, they were not identical.

Having said as much as this, I go further, and maintain that the word "consulted," used as it was used, was in no respect unadvisable, except so far as it distressed any learned and good men, who identified it with the Latin. I might, indeed, even have defended the word as it was used, in the Latin sense of it. Regnier both uses it of the laity and explains it. "Cùm receptam apud populos traditionem *consulunt* et *sequuntur* Episcopi, non illos habent pro magistris et ducibus, &c." (*De Eccles. Christ.* p. i. §1, c. i., ed. Migne, col. 234) But in my bountifulness I will give up this use of the word as untheological; still I will maintain that the true theological sense is unknown to all *but* theologians. Accordingly, the use of it in the *Rambler* was in no sense dangerous to any lay reader, who, if he knows Latin, still is not called upon, in the structure of his religious ideas, to draw those careful lines and those fine distinctions, which in theology itself are the very means of anticipating and repelling heresy. The laity would not have a truer, or a clearer, or a different view of doctrine itself, though the sentence had run, "in the preparation of a dogmatic decree, *regard* is had to the sense of the faithful;" or, "there is an *appeal* to the general voice of the faithful;" or, "*inquiry* is made into the belief of the Christian people;" or, "the definition is not made without a previous *reference* to what the faithful will think of it and say to it;" or though any other form of words had been used, stronger or weaker, expressive of the same general idea, viz. that *the sense of the faithful is not left out of the question* by the Holy See among the preliminary acts of defining a doctrine.

Now I shall go on presently to remark on the proposition itself which is conveyed in the words on which I have been commenting; here, however, I will first observe, that such misconceptions as I have been setting right will and must occur, from the nature of the case, whenever we speak on theological subjects in the vernacular; and if we do not use the vernacular, I do not see how the bulk of the Catholic people are to be catechised or taught at all. English has innovated on the Latin sense of its own Latin words; and if we are to speak according to the conditions of the language, and are to make ourselves intelligible to the multitude, we shall necessarily run the risk of startling those who are resolved to act as mere critics and scholastics in the process of popular instruction.

This divergence from a classical or ecclesiastical standard is a great inconvenience, I grant; but we cannot remodel our mother-tongue. *Crimen* does not properly mean *crime; amiable* does not yet convey the idea of *amabilis; compassio* is not *compassion; princeps* is not a *prince; disputatio* is not *a dispute; praevenire* is not to *prevent. Cicero imperator* is not *the Emperor Cicero; scriptor egregius* is not *an egregious writer; virgo singularis* is not *a singular virgin; retractare dicta* is not *to retract what he has said;* and, as we know from the sacred passage, *traducere* is not necessarily *to traduce.*

Now this is not merely sharp writing, for mistakes do in matter of fact occur not infrequently from this imperfect correspondence between theological Latin and English; showing that readers of English are bound ever to bear in mind that they are not reading Latin, and that learned divines must ever exercise charity in their interpretations of vernacular religious teaching.

For instance, I know of certain English sermons which were translated into French by some French priests. They, good and friendly men, were surprised to find in these compositions such language as "weak evidence and strong evidence," and "insufficient, probably, demonstrative evidence"; they read that "some writers had depreciated the evidences of religion," and that "the last century, when love was cold, was an age of evidences." *Evidentia*, they said, meant that luminousness which attends on demonstration, conviction, certainty; how can it be more or less? how can it be unsatisfactory? how can a sane man disparage it? how can it be connected with religious coldness? The simple explanation of the difficulty was, that the writer was writing for his own people, and that in English "an evidence" is not *evidentia*.

Another instance. An excellent Italian religious, now gone to his reward, was reading a work of the same author; and he came upon a sentence to the effect, I think, that the doctrine of the Holy Trinity was to be held with "implicit" faith. He was perplexed and concerned. He thought the writer held that the Church did not explicitly teach, had not explicitly defined, the dogma; that is, he confused the English meaning of the word, according to which it is a sort of correlative to *imperative,* meaning simple, unconditional, absolute, with its sense in theology.

It is not so exactly apposite to refer,—yet I will refer,—to another instance, as supplying a general illustration of the point I am urging. It was in a third country that a lecturer spoke in terms of disparagement of "Natural Theology," on the ground of its deciding questions of revelation by reasonings from physical phenomena. It was objected to him, that *Naturalis Theologia* embraced *all* truths and arguments from natural reason bearing upon the Divine Being and Attributes. Certainly he would have been the last to depreciate what he had ever made the paramount preliminary science to Christian faith; but he spoke according to the sense of those to whom his words might come. He considered that in the Protestant school of Paley and other popular writers, the idea of Natural Theology had practically merged in a scientific view of the argument from Design.

Once more. Supposing a person were to ask me whether a friend, who has told me the fact in confidence, had written a certain book, and I were to answer, "Well, if he did, he certainly would tell *me*," and the inquirer went away satisfied that he did *not* write it,—I do not see that I have done any thing to incur the reproach of the English word "equivocation;" I have but adopted a mode of turning off a difficult question, to which any one may be obliged any day to have recourse. I am not speaking of spontaneous and gratuitous assertions, statements on solemn occasions, or answers to formal authorities. I am speaking of impertinent or unjustifiable questions; and I should like to know the man who thinks himself bound to say every thing to every one. Physicians evade the questions of sick persons about themselves; friends break bad news gradually, and with temporary concealments, to those whom it may shock. Parents shuffle with their children. Statesmen, ministers in Parliament, baffle adversaries in every possible way short of a direct infringement of veracity. When St. Athanasius saw that he was pursued on the Nile by the imperial officers, he turned round his boat and met them; when they came up to his party and hailed them, and asked whether they had seen any thing of Athanasius, Athanasius cried out, "O yes, he is not far from you:" and off the vessels went in different directions as swiftly as they could go, each boat on its own errand, the pursuer and the pursued. I do not see that there is in any of these instances what is expressed by the English word "equivocation;" but it *is* the *equivocatio* of a Latin treatise; and when

Protestants hear that *aequivocamus sine scrupulo*, they are shocked at the notion of our "unscrupulous equivocation."

Now, in saying all this, I must not be supposed to be forgetful of the sacred and imperative duty of preserving with religious exactness all those theological terms which are ecclesiastically recognized as portions of dogmatic statements, such as *Trinity, Person, Consubstantial, Nature, Transubstantiation, Sacrament,* &c. It would be unpardonable for a Catholic to teach "justification by faith only," and say that he meant by "faith" *fides formata,* or "justification without works," and say that he meant by "works" the works of the Jewish ritual; but granting all this fully, still if our whole religious phraseology is, as matter of duty, to be modelled in strict conformity to theological Latin, neither the poor nor children will understand us. I have always fancied that to preachers great license was allowed, not only in the wording, but even in the matter of their discourses: they exaggerate and are rhetorical, and they are understood *piè* as speaking *more praedicatorio.* I have always fancied that, when Catholics were accused of hyperbolical language towards the Blessed Virgin, it was replied that devotion was not the measure of doctrine; nor surely is the vernacular of a magazine writer. I do not see that I am wrong in considering that a periodical, not treating theology *ex professo,* but accidentally alluding to an ecclesiastical act, commits no real offence if it uses an unscientific word, since it speaks, not *more digladiatorio,* but *colloquialiter.*

I shall conclude this head of my subject with allusion to a passage in the history of St. Dionysius the Great, Bishop of Alexandria, though it is beyond my purpose; but I like to quote a saint whom, *multis nominibus* (not "with many names," or "by many *nouns*"), I have always loved most of all the Ante-Nicene Fathers. It relates to an attack which

was made on his orthodoxy; a very serious matter. Now I
know every one will be particular on his own special
science or pursuits. I am the last man to find fault with
such particularity. Drill-sergeants think much of deport-
ment; hard logicians come down with a sledge-hammer
even on a Plato who does not happen to enumerate in his
beautiful sentences all the argumentative considerations
which go to make up his conclusion; scholars are horrified,
as if with sensible pain, at the perpetration of a false
quantity. I am far from ridiculing, despising, or even under-
valuing such precision; it is for the good of every art and
science that it should have vigilant guardians. Nor am I
comparing such precision (far from it) with that true
religious zeal which leads theologians to keep the sacred
Ark of the Covenant in every letter of its dogma, as a
tremendous deposit for which they are responsible. In this
curious sceptical world, such sensitiveness is the only
human means by which the treasure of faith can be kept
inviolate. There is a woe in Scripture against the unfaithful
shepherd. We do not blame the watch-dog because he
sometimes flies at the wrong person. I conceive the force,
the peremptoriness, the sternness, with which the Holy
See comes down upon the vagrant or the robber, tres-
passing upon the enclosure of revealed truth, is the only
sufficient antagonist to the power and subtlety of the
world, to imperial comprehensiveness, monarchical sel-
fishness, nationalism, the liberalism of philosophy, the
encroachments and usurpations of science. I grant, I maintain all this; and after this avowal, lest I be misunderstood,
I venture to introduce my notice of St. Dionysius. He was
accused on a far worse charge, and before a far more
formidable tribunal, than commonly befalls a Catholic
writer; for he was brought up before the Holy See on a
denial of our Lord's divinity. He had been controverting

with the Sabellians; and he was in consequence accused of the doctrine to which Arius afterwards gave his name, that is, of considering our Lord a creature. He says, writing in his defence, that when he urged his opponents with the argument that "a vine and a vine-dresser were not the same," neither, therefore, were the "Father and the Son," these were not the only illustrations that he made use of, nor those on which he dwelt, for he also spoke of "a root and a plant," "a fount and a stream," which are not only *distinct* from each other, but of one and the same *nature*. Then he adds, "But my accusers have no eyes to see this portion of my treatise; but they take up two little words detached from the context, and proceed to discharge them at me as pebbles from a sling."[1] If even a saint's words are not always precise enough to allow of being made a dogmatic text, much less are those of any modern periodical.

The conclusion I would draw from all I have been saying is this: Without deciding whether or not it is advisable to introduce points of theology into popular works, and especially whether it is advisable for laymen to do so, still, if this actually *is* done, we are not to expect in them that perfect accuracy of expression which is demanded in a Latin treatise or a lecture *ex cathedrâ;* and if there be a want of this exactness, we must not at once think it proceeds from self-will and undutifulness in the writers.

2

Now I come to the *matter* of what the writer in the *Rambler* really said, putting aside the question of the *wording;* and I begin by expressing my belief that, what-

1 Athan. de Sent. Dion. 8.

ever he may be willing to admit on the score of theological
Latinity in the use of the word "consult" when applied to
the faithful, yet one thing he cannot deny, viz. that in
using it, he implied, from the very force of the term, that
they are treated by the Holy See, on occasions such as
that specified, with attention and consideration.

Then follows the question, Why? and the answer is
plain, viz. because the body of the faithful is one of the
witnesses to the fact of the tradition of revealed doctrine,
and because their *consensus* through Christendom is the
voice of the Infallible Church.

I think I am right in saying that the tradition of the
Apostles, committed to the whole Church in its various
constituents and function *per modum unius,* manifests
itself variously at various times: sometimes by the mouth
of the episcopacy, sometimes by the doctors, sometimes
by the people, sometimes by liturgies, rites, ceremonies,
and customs, by events, disputes, movements, and all
those other phenomena which are comprised under the
name of history. It follows that none of these channels of
tradition may be treated with disrespect; granting at the
same time fully, that the gift of discerning, discriminating,
defining, promulgating, and enforcing any portion of that
tradition resides solely in the *Ecclesia docens.*

One man will lay more stress on one aspect of doctrine,
another on another; for myself, I am accustomed to lay
great stress on the *consensus fidelium,* and I will say how
it has to come about.

1. It had long been to me a difficulty, that I could
not find certain portions of the defined doctrine of the
Church in ecclesiastical writers. I was at Rome in the
year 1847; and then I had the great advantage and honour
of seeing Fathers Perrone and Passaglia, and having
various conversations with them on this point. The point

of difficulty was this, that up to the date of the definition of certain articles of doctrine respectively, there was so very deficient evidence from existing documents that Bishops, doctors, theologians, held them. I do not mean to say that I expressed my difficulty in this formal shape; but that what passed between us in such interviews as they were kind enough to give me, ran into or impinged upon this question. Nor would I ever dream of making them answerable for the impression which their answers made on me; but, speaking simply on my own responsibility, I should say that, while Father Passaglia seemed to maintain that the Ante-Nicene writers were clear in their testimonies in behalf (*e.g.*) of the doctrines of the Holy Trinity and Justification, expressly praising and making much of the Anglican Bishop Bull; Father Perrone, on the other hand, not speaking, indeed directly upon those particular doctrines, but rather on such as I will presently introduce in his own words, seemed to me to say "*transeat*" to the alleged fact which constituted the difficulty, and to lay a great stress on which he considered to be the *sensus and consensus fidelium,* as a compensation for whatever deficiency there might be of patristical testimony in behalf of various points of the Catholic dogma.

2. I should have been led to fancy, perhaps, that he was shaping his remarks in the direction in which he considered he might be especially serviceable to myself, who had been accustomed to account for the (supposed) phenomena in another way, had it not been for his work on the Immaculate Conception, which I read the next year with great interest, and which was passing through the press when I saw him. I am glad to have this opportunity of expressing my gratitude and attachment to a venerable man, who never grudged me his valuable time.

But now for his treatise, to which I have referred, so
far as it speaks of the *sensus fidelium,* and of its bearing
upon the doctrine, of which his work treats, and upon its
definition.

(1.) He states the historical *fact* of such *sensus.* Speaking of the "Ecclesiae sensus" on the subject, he says that,
though the liturgies of the Feast of the Conception "satis
apertè patefaciant quid Ecclesia antiquitùs de hoc senserit
argumento," yet it may be worth while to add some direct
remarks on the sense itself of the Church. Then he says,
"Ex duplici fonte eum colligi posse arbitramur, tum
scilicet ex pastorum, *tum ex fidelium* sese gerendi ratione"
(pp. 74, 75). Let it be observed, he not only joins together the *pastores* and *fideles,* but contrasts them; I mean
(for it will bear on what is to follow), the "faithful" do
not *include* the "pastors."

(2.) Next he goes on to describe the relation of that
sensus fidelium to the *sensus Ecclesiae.* He says, that to
inquire into the sense of the Church on any question, is
nothing else but to investigate towards which side of it
she has more inclined. And the "indicia et manifestationes
hujus propensionis" are her public acts, liturgies, feasts,
prayers, "pastorum ac *fidelium* in unum veluti conspiratio"
(p. 101). Again, at p. 109, joining together in one this
twofold consent of pastors and people, he speaks of the
"unanimis pastorum ac *fidelium* consensio . . . per liturgias,
per festa, per euchologia, per fidei controversias, per
conciones patefacta."

(3.) These various "indicia" are also the *instrumenta
traditionis,* and vary one with another in the evidence
which they give in favour of paticular doctrines; so that
the strength of one makes up in a particular case for the
deficiency of another, and the strength of the "sensus

communis fidelium" can make up (*e.g.*) for the the silence of the Fathers. "Istiusmodi instrumenta interdum simul conjunctè conspirare possunt ad traditionem aliquam apostolicam atque divinam patefaciendam, interdum vero seorsum.... Perperam nonnulli solent ad inficiandam traditionis alicujus existentiam urgere silentium Patrum ... quid enim si silentium istud alio pacto ... compensetur?" (p. 139). He instances this from St. Irenaeus and Tertullian in the "Successio Episcoporum," who transmit the doctrines "tum activi operâ ministerii, tum usu et praxi, tum institutis ritibus ... adeò ut catholica atque apostolica doctrina inoculata ... fuerit ... communi Ecclesiae coetui" (p. 142).

(4.) He then goes on to speak directly of the force of the "sensus fidelium," as distinct (not separate) from the teaching of their pastors. "*Praestantissimi* theologi maximam *probandi* vim huic communi sensui inesse *uno ore* fatentur. Etenim Canus, 'In quaestione fidei,' inquit, 'communis fidelis populi sensus haud levem facit fidem' " (p. 143). He gives another passage from him in a note, which he introduces with the words, "Illud *praeclarè* addit;" what Canus adds is, "Quaero ex te, quando de rebus Christanae fidei inter nos contendimus, non de philosophiae decretis, utrùm potius *quaerendum* est, quid philosophi atque ethnici, an quid homines Christiani, et *doctriná et fide* instituti, *sentiant?*" Now certainly "quaerere quid sentiant homines doctrinâ et fide instituti," though not asking advice, is an act implying not a little deference on the part of the persons addressing towards the parties addressed.

Father Perrone continues, "Gregorius verò de Valentiâ fusius vim ejusmodi fidelium consensus evolvit. 'Est enim,' inquit, 'in *definitionibus fidei* habenda ratio, quoad fieri potest, consensus fidelium.' " Here, again, "habere ration-

em," to have regard to, is an act of respect and consideration. However, Gregory continues, "Quoniam *et ii* sanè,
quatenus *ex ipsis* constat Ecclesia, sic *Spiritu Sancto
assistente,* divinas revelationes *integrè et purè conservant,*
ut omnes illi quidem aberrare non possunt.... Illud solùm
contendo: Si quando de re aliquâ *in materie religionis* con-
troversia (controversa?) constaret fidelium omnium con-
cordem esse sententiam (solet autem id constare, vel ex
ipsâ praxi alicujus cultus communiter apud christianos
populos receptâ, vel ex *scandalo et offensione communi,*
quae opinione aliquâ oritur, &c.) meritò *posse et debere*
Pontificem illâ *niti,* ut quae esset *Ecclesiae sententia in-
fallibilis"* (p. 144). Thus Gregory says that, in controversy
about a matter of faith, the consent of all the faithful has
such a force in the proof of this side or that, that the
Supreme Pontiff *is able and ought* to *rest* upon it, as
being the *judgment or sentiment* of the *infallible* Church.
These are surely exceedingly strong words; not that I take
them to mean strictly that infallibility is *in* the "consensus fidelium," but that that "consensus" is an *indicium*
or *instrumentum* to us of the judgement of that Church
which *is* infallible.

Father Perrone proceeds to quote from Petavius, who
supplies us with the following striking admonition from
St. Paulinus, viz. "ut de omnium fidelium *ore pendeamus,*
quia in omnem fidelem Spiritus Dei spirat."

Petavius speaks thus, as he quotes him (p. 156):
"*Movet me,* ut in eam (viz. piam) sententiam sim pro-
pensior, *communis maximus sensus fidelium omnium.*"
By "movet me" he means, that he *attends* to what the
coetus fidelium says: this is certainly not passing over the
fideles, but making much of them.

In a later part of his work (p. 186), Father Perrone
speaks of the "consensus fidelium" under the strong image

of a *seal*. After mentioning various arguments in favour of the Immaculate Conception, such as the testimony of so many universities, religious bodies, theologians, &c., he continues, "Haec demum omnia firmissimo veluti *sigillo obsignat* totius christiani populi consensus."

(5.) He proceeds to give several instances, in which the definition of doctrine was made in consequence of nothing else but the "sensus fidelium" and the "juge et vivum magisterium" of the Church.

For his meaning of the "juge et vivum magisterium Ecclesiae," he refers us to his *Praelectiones* (part ii. 2, c. ii.). In that passage I do not see that he defines the sense of the word; but I understand him to mean that high authoritative voice or act which is the Infallible Church's prerogative, inasmuch as she is the teacher of the nations; and which is a sufficient warrant to all men for a doctrine being true and being *de fide*, by the fact of its formally occurring. It is distinct from, and independent of, tradition, though never in fact separated from it. He says, "Fit ut traditio dogmatica identificetur cum ipsâ Ecclesiae doctrinâ, a quâ separari nequit; qua propter, *etsi documenta deficerent omnia*, solum hoc vivum et juge magisterium *satis esset* ad cognoscendam doctrinam divinitus traditam, habito praesertim respectu ad solemnes Christi promissiones" (p. 303).

This being understood, he speaks of several points of faith which have been determined and defined by the "magisterium" of the Church and, as to tradition, on the "consensus fidelium," prominently, if no solely.

The most remarkable of these is the "dogma de visione Dei beatificâ" possessed by souls after purgatory and before the day of judgment; a point which Protestants, availing themselves of the comment of the Benedictines of St. Maur upon St. Ambrose, are accustomed to urge

in controversy. "Nemo est qui nesciat," says Father
Perrone, "quot utriusque Ecclesiae, tum Graecae tum
Latinae, Patres contrarium sensisse visi sunt" (p. 147). He
quotes in a note the words of the Benedictine editor, as
follows: "Propemodum incredibile videri potest, quàm in
eâ quaestione sancti Patres ab ipsis Apostolorum temporibus ad Gregorii XI. (Benedicti XII) pontificatum
florentinumque concilium, hoc est toto quatuordecim
seculorum spatio, incerti ac parùm constantes exstiterint."
Father Perrone continues: "Certè quidem in Ecclesiâ non
deerat quoad hunc fidei articulum divina traditio; alioquin
nunquam is definiri potuisset: verùm non omnibus illa
erat comperta; divina eloquia haud satis in re sunt conspicua; *Patres*, ut vidimus, in varias abierunt sententias;
liturgiae ipsae non modicam prae se ferunt difficultatem.
His omnibus succurrit juge Ecclesiae magisterium, *communis praeterea fidelium sensus;* qui altè adeò defixum . . .
habebant mentibus, purgatas animas statim ad Deum
videndum eoque fruendum admitti, ut non minimum
eorum animi vel ex ipsâ controvesiâ fuerint *offensi*, quae
sub Joanne XXII. agitabatur, et cujus definitio *diu nimis
protrahebatur.*" Now does not this imply that the tradition,
on which the definition was made, was manifested in the
consensus fidelium with a luminousness which the succession of Bishops, though many of them were "Sancti Patres
ab ipsis Apostolorum temporibus," did not furnish? that
the definition was delayed till the *fideles* would bear the
delay no longer? that it was made because of them and
for their sake, because of their strong feelings? If so, surely,
in plain English, most considerable deference was paid
to the "sensus fidelium;" their opinion and advice indeed
was not asked, but their testimony was taken, their feelings
consulted, their impatience, I had almost said, feared.

In like manner, as regards the doctrine, though not the

definition, of the Immaculate Conception, he says, not denying, of course, the availableness of the other "instrumenta traditionis" in this particular case, "Ratissimum est, Christi fideles omnes circa hunc articulum unius esse animi, idque ita, ut maximo afficerentur *scandalo*, si vel minima de Immaculatâ Virginis Conceptione quaestio moveretur" (p. 156).

3. A year had hardly passed from the appearance of Fr. Perrone's book in England, when the Pope published his Encyclical Letter. In it he asked the Bishops of the Catholic world, "ut nobis significare velitis, quâ devotione vester clerus *populusque fidelis* erga Immaculatae Virginis conceptionem sit animatus et quo desiderio flagret, ut ejusmodi res ab apostolicâ sede decernatur;" that is, when it came to the point to take measures for the definition of the doctrine, he did lay a special stress on this particular preliminary, viz. the ascertainment of the feeling of the faithful both towards the doctrine and its definition; as the *Rambler* stated in the passage out of which this argument has arisen. It seems to me important to keep this in view, whatever becomes of the word "consulted," which, I have already said, is not to be taken in its ordinary Latin sense.

4. At length, in 1854, the definition took place, and the Pope's Bull containing it made its appearance. In it the Holy Father speaks as he had spoken in his Encyclical, viz. that although he *already* knew the sentiments of the Bishops, still he had wished to know the sentiments of the *people* also: "*Quamvis* nobis ex receptis postulationibus de definiendâ tandem aliquando Immacultâ Virginis Conceptione *perspectus* esset plurimorum sociorum *Antistitum* sensus, tamen Encyclicas literas, &c. ad omnes Ven. FF. totius Catholici orbis sacrorum Antistites misimus, ut, adhibitis ad Deum precibus, nobis scripto *etiam* significa-

rent, quae esset suorum *fidelium* erga Immaculatam Dei-
parae Conceptionem pietas et devotio," &c. And when,
before the formal definition, he enumerates the various
witnesses to the apostolicity of the doctrine, he sets down
"divina eloquia, veneranda traditio, perpetuus Ecclesiae
sensus, singularis catholicorum Antistitum ac *fidelium* conspiratio. *Conspiratio;* the two, the Church teaching and
the Church taught, are put together, as one twofold testimony, illustrating each other, and never to be divided.

5. A year or two passed, and the Bishop of Birmingham
published his treatise on the doctrine. I close this portion
of my paper with an extract from his careful view of the
argument. "Nor should the universal conviction of pious
Catholics be passed over, as of small account in the general
argument; for that pious belief, and the devotion which
springs from it, are the *faithful reflection* of the pastoral
teaching" (p. 172). Reflection; that is, the people are a
mirror, in which the Bishops see themselves. Well, I suppose a person may *consult* his glass, and in that way may
know things about himself which he can learn in no other
way. This is what Fr. Perrone above seems to say has sometimes actually been the case, as in the instance of the
"beatifica visio" of the saints; at least he does not mention
the *"pastorum* ac fidelium *conspiratio"* in reviewing the
grounds of its definition, but simply the "juge Ecclesiae
magisterium" and the "communis fidelium sensus."

His lordship proceeds: "The more devout the faithful
grew, the more devoted they showed themselves towards
this mystery. And it is the devout who have the surest instinct in discerning the mysteries of which the Holy Spirit
breathes the grace through the Church, and who, with as
sure a tact, reject what is alien from her teaching. The
common accord of the faithful has weight much as an
argument even with the most learned divines. St. Augus-

tine says, that amongst many things which most justly held him in the bosom of the Catholic Church, was the 'accord of populations and of nations.' In another work he says, 'It seems that I have believed nothing but the confirmed opinion and the exceedingly wide-spread report of populations and of nations.' Elsewhere he says: 'In matters whereupon the Scripture has not spoken clearly, the custom of the people of God, or the institutions of our predecessors, are to be held as law.' In the same spirit St. Jerome argues, whilst defending the use of relics against Vigilantius: 'So the people of all the Churches who have gone out to meet holy relics, and have received them with so much joy, are to be accounted foolish'" (pp. 172, 173).

And here I might come to an end; but, having got so far, I am induced, before concluding, to suggest an historical instance of the same great principle, which Father Perrone does not draw out.

3

First, I will set down the various ways in which theologians put before us the bearing of the Consent of the faithful upon the manifestation of the tradition of the Church. Its *consensus* is to be regarded: 1. as a testimony to the fact of the apostolical dogma; 2. as a sort of instinct, or *PHRONĒMA* deep in the bosom of the mystical body of Christ; 3. as a direction of the Holy Ghost; 4. as an answer to its prayer; 5. as a jealousy of error, which it at once feels as a scandal.

1. The first of these I need not enlarge upon, as it is illustrated in the foregoing passages from Father Perrone.

2. The second is explained in the well-known passages of Möhler's *Symbolique;* e.g. "L'esprit de Dieu, qui gouverne et vivifie L'Eglise, enfante dans l'homme, en s'unis-

sant à lui, *un instinct,* un tact éminemment chrètien, qui le conduit â toute craie doctrine. . . . Ce sentiment commun, cette conscience de l'Eglise est la tradition dans le sens subjectif du mot. Qu'est-ce donc que la tradition considérée sous ce point de vue? C'est le sens chrétien existant dans l'Eglise, et transmis par l'Eglise; sens, toutefois, qu'on ne peut séparer des vérités qu'il contient, puisqu'il est formé de ces vérités et par ces vérités." Ap. Perrone, p. 142.

3. Cardinal Fisher seems to speak of the third, as he is quoted by Petavius, *De Incarn.* xiv. 2; that is, he speaks of a custom imperceptibly gaining a position, "nullâ praeceptorum vi, sed consensu quodam tacito tam populi quàm cleri, quasi tacitis omnium suffragiis recepta fuit, priusquàm ullo conciliorum decreto legimus eam fuisse firmatam." And then he adds, "This custom has its birth *in that people which is ruled by the Holy Ghost,*" &c.

4. Petavius speaks of a fourth aspect of it. "It is well said by St. Augustine, that to the minds of individuals certain things are revealed by God, not only by extraordinary means, as in visions, &c., but also in those usual ways, according to which what is unknown to them is opened *in answer to their prayer.* After this manner it is to be believed that God has revealed to Christians the sinless Conception of the Immaculate Virgin." *De Incarn.* xiv. 2, 11.

5. The fifth is enlarged upon in Dr. Newman's second *Lecture on Anglican Difficulties,* from which I quote a few lines: "We know that it is the property of life to be impatient of any foreign substance in the body to which it belongs. It will be sovereign in its own domain, and it conflicts with what it cannot assimilate into itself, and *is irritated and disordered* till it has expelled it. Such expulsion, then, is emphatically a test of uncongeniality, for it shows

that the substance ejected, not only is not one with the body that rejects it, but cannot be made one with it; that its introduction is not only useless, or superfluous, or adventitious, but that it is intolerable." Presently he continues: "The religious life of a people is of a certain quality and direction, and these are tested by the mode in which it encounters the various opinions, customs, and institutions which are submitted to it. Drive a stake into a river's bed, and you will at once ascertain which way it is running, and at what speed; throw up even a straw upon the air, and you will see which way the wind blows; submit your heretical and Catholic principle to the action of the multitude, and you will be able to pronounce at once whether it is imbued with Catholic truth or with heretical falsehood." And then he proceeds to exemplify this by a passage in the history of Arianism, the very history which I intend now to take, as illustrative of the truth and importance of the thesis on which I am insisting.

It is not a little remarkable, that, though historically speaking, the fourth century is the age of doctors, illustrated, as it was, by the saints Athanasius, Hilary, the two Gregories, Basil, Chrysostom, Ambrose, Jerome, and Augustine, and all of these saints bishops also, except one, nevertheless in that very day the divine tradition committed to the infallible Church was proclaimed and maintained far more by the faithful than by the Episcopate.

Here, of course, I must explain:—in saying this, then, undoubtedly I am not denying that the great body of the Bishops were in their internal belief orthodox; nor that there were numbers of clergy who stood by the laity, and acted as their centres and guides; nor that the laity actually received their faith, in the first instance, from the Bishops and clergy; nor that some portions of the laity were ignorant, and other portions at length corrupted by the Arian teachers, who got possession of the sees and ordained an heretical clergy;—but I mean still, that in that time of immense confusion the divine dogma of our Lord's divinity was proclaimed, enforced, maintained, and (humanly speaking) preserved, far more by the "Ecclesia docta" than by the "Ecclesia docens;" that the body of the episcopate was unfaithful to its commission, while the body of the laity was faithful to its baptism; that at one time the Pope, at other times the patriarchal, metropolitan, and other great sees, at other times general councils, said what they should not have said, or did what obscured and compromised revealed truth; while, on the other hand, it was the Christian people who, under Providence, were the ecclesiastical strength of Athanasius, Hilary, Eusebius of Vercellae, and other great solitary confessors, who would have failed without them.

I see, then, in the Arian history a palmary example of a state of the Church, during which, in order to know the tradition of the Apostles, we must have recourse to the faithful; for I fairly own, that if I go to writers, since I must adjust the letter of Justin, Clement, and Hippolytus with the Nicene Doctors, I get confused; and what revives and reinstates me, as far as history goes, is the faith of the people. For I argue that unless they had been catechised, as St. Hilary says, in the orthodox faith from the time of their baptism, they never could have had that horror, which they show, of the heterodox Arian doctrine. Their voice, then, is the voice of tradition; and the instance comes to us with still greater emphasis, when we consider —1. that it occurs in the very beginning of the history of the "Ecclesia docens," for there can scarcely be said to be any history of her teaching till the age of martyrs was over; 2. that the doctrine in controversy was so momentous, being the very foundation of the Christian system; 3. that the state of controversy and disorder lasted over the long space of sixty years; and 4. that it involved serious persecutions, in life, limb, and property, to the faithful whose loyal perseverance decided it.

It seems, then, as striking an instance as I could take in fulfilment of Father Perrone's statement, that the voice of tradition may in certain cases express itself, not by Councils, nor Fathers, nor Bishops, but the "communis fidelium sensus."

I shall set down some authorities for the two points successively, which I have to enforce, viz. that the Nicene dogma was maintained during the greater part of the 4th century,

1. not by the unswerving firmness of the Holy See, Councils, or Bishops, but

2. by the "consensus fidelium."

I. On the one hand, then, I say, that there was a temporary suspense of the functions of the "Ecclesia docens." The body of Bishops failed in their confession of the faith. They spoke variously, one against another; there was nothing, after Nicaea, of firm, unvarying, consistent testimony, for nearly sixty years. There were untrustworthy Councils, unfaithful Bishops; there was weakness, fear of consequences, misguidance, delusion, hallucination, endless, hopeless, extending itself into nearly every corner of the Catholic Church. The comparatively few who remained faithful were discredited and driven into exile; the rest were either deceivers or were deceived.

1. A.D. 325. The great council of Nicaea, of 318 Bishops, chiefly from the eastern provinces of Christendom, under the presidency of Hosius of Cordova, as the Pope's Legate. It was convoked against Arainism, which it once for all anathematized; and it inserted the formula of the "Consubstantial" into the Creed, with the view of

establishing the fundamental dogma which Arianism impugned. It is the first Oecumenical Council, and recognised at the time its own authority as the voice of the infallible Church. It is so received by the *orbis terrarum* at this day.

The history of the Arian controversy, from its date, A.D. 325, to the date of the second Oecumenical Council, A.D. 381, is the history of the struggle through Christendom for the universal acceptance or the repudiation of the formula of the "Consubstantial."

2. A.D. 334, 335. The synods of Caesarea and Tyre against Athanasius, who was therein accused and formally condemned of rebellion, sedition, and ecclesiastical tyranny; of murder, sacrilege, and magic; deposed from his see, forbidden to set foot in Alexandria for life, and banished to Gaul. Constantine confirmed the sentence.

3. A.D. 341. Council of Rome of fifty Bishops, attended by the exiles from Thrace, Syria, &c., by Athanasius, &c., in which Athanasius was pronounced innocent.

4. A.D. 341. Great Council of the Dedication at Antioch, attended by ninety or a hundred Bishops. The council ratified the proceedings of the councils of Caesarea and Tyre, and placed an Arian in the see of Athanasius. Then it proceeded to pass a dogmatic decree in reversal of the formula of the "Consubstantial." Four or five creeds, instead of the Nicene, were successively adopted by the assembled fathers. The first was a creed which they ascribed to Lucian, a martyr and saint of the preceding century, in whom the Arians always gloried as their master. The second was fuller and stronger in its language, and made more pretension to ortodoxy. The third was more feeble again. These three creeds were circulated in the neighbourbood; but, as they wished to send one to Rome, they directed a fourth to be drawn up. This, too,

apparently failed. So little was known at the time of the real history of this synod and its creeds, that St. Hilary calls it "sanctorum synodus."

5. A.D. 345. Council of the creed called Macrostich. This creed suppresses, as did the third, the word "substance." The eastern Bishops sent this to the Bishops of the West, who rejected it.

6. A.D. 347. The great council of Sardica, attended by 380 Bishops. Before it commenced, the division between its members broke out on the question whether or not Athanasius should have a seat in it. In consequence, seventy-six retired to Philippopolis, on the Thracian side of Mount Haemus, and there excommunicated the Pope and the Sardican fathers. These seceders published a sixth confession of faith. The synod of Sardica, including Bishops from Italy, Gaul, Africa, Egypt, Cyprus, and Palestine, confirmed the act of the Roman council, and restored Athanasius and the other exiles to their sees. The synod of Philippopolis, on the contrary, sent letters to the civil magistrates of those cities, forbidding them to admit the exiles into them. The imperial power took part with the Sardican fathers, and Athanasius went back to Alexandria.

7. A.D. 351. Before many years had run out, the great eastern party was up again.

Under pretence of putting down a kind of Sabellianism, they drew up a new creed, into which they introduced certain inadvisable expressions of some of the ante-Nicene writers, on the subject of our Lord's divinity, and dropped the word "substance." St. Hilary thought this creed also Catholic; and other Catholic writers style its fathers "holy Bishops."

8. There is considerable confusion of dates here. Anyhow, there was a second Sirmian creed, in which the

eastern party first came to a division among themselves.
St. Hilary at length gives up these creeds as indefensible,
and calls this one a "blasphemy." It is the first creed which
criticises the words "substance," &c., as unscriptural. Some
years afterwards this "blasphemia" seems to have been
interpolated, and sent into the East in the name of Hosius.
At a later date, there was a third Sirmian creed; and a
second edition of it, with alterations, was published at Nice
in Thrace.

    9. A.D. 353. The council of Arles. I cannot find how
many Bishops attended it. As the Pope sent several Bishops
as legates, it must have been one of great importance. The
Bishop of Arles was an Arian, and managed to seduce, or
to force, a number of orthodox Bishops, including the
Pope's legate, Vincent, to subscribe the condemnation of
Athanasius. Paulinus, Bishop of Trêves, was nearly the
only champion of the Nicene faith and of Athanasius. He
was accordingly banished into Phrygia, where he died.

    10. A.D. 355. The council of Milan, of more than 300
Bishops of the West. Nearly all of them, subscribed the
condemnation of Athanasius; whether they generally subscribed the heretical creed, which was brought forward,
does not appear. The Pope's four legates remained firm,
and St. Dionysius of Milan, who died an exile in Asia
Minor. An Arian was put into his see. Saturninus, the
Bishop of Arles, proceeded to hold a council at Beziers;
and its fathers banished St. Hilary to Phrygia.

    11. A.D. 357. Hosius falls. "Constantius used such
violence towards the old man, and confined him so straitly,
that at last, broken by suffering, he was brought, though
hardly, to hold communion with Valens and Ursacius
(the Arian leaders), though he would not subscribe
against Athanasius." Athan, *Arian. Hist.* 45.

    12. Liberius. A.D. 357 "The tragedy was not ended in

the lapse of Hosius, but in the evil which befell Liberius, the Roman Pontiff, it became far more dreadful and mournful, considering that he was Bishop of so great a city, and of the whole Catholic Church, and that he had so bravely resisted Constantius two years previously. There is nothing, whether in the historians and holy fathers, or in his own letters, to prevent our coming to the conclusion, that Liberius communicated with the Arians, and confirmed the sentence passed against Athanasius; but he is not at all on that account to be called a heretic." Baron. Ann. 357, 38-45. Athanasius says: "Liberius, after he had been in banishment for two years, gave way, and from fear of threatened death was induced to subscribe." *Arian. Hist.* 41. St. Jerome says: "Liberius, taedio victus exilii, in haereticam pravitatem subscribens, Roman quasi victor intraverat." *Chron.*

13. A.D. 359. The great councils of Seleucia and Ariminum, being one bi-partite council, representing the East and West respectively. At Seleucia there were 150 Bishops, of which only the twelve or thirteen from Egypt were champions of the Nicene "Consubstantial." At Ariminum there were as many as 400 Bishops, who, worn out by the artifice of long delay on the part of the Arians, abandoned the "Consubstantial," and subscribed the ambiguous formula which the heretics had substituted for it.

14. A.D. 361. The death of Constantius; the Catholic Bishops breathe again, and begin at once to remedy the miseries of the Church, though troubles were soon to break out anew.

15. A.D. 362. State of the Church of Antioch at this time. There were four Bishops or communions of Antioch; first, the old succession and communion, which had possession before the Arian troubles; secondly, the Arian succession, which had lately conformed to orthodoxy in

the person of Meletius; thirdly, the new Latin succession, lately created by Lucifer, whom some have thought the Pope's legate there; and, fourthly, the new Arian succession, which was begun upon the recantation of Meletius. At length, as Arianism was brought under, the evil reduced itself to two successions, that of Meletius and the Latin, which went on for many years, the West and Egypt holding communion with the latter, and the East with the former.

16. A.D. 370-379. St. Basil was Bishop of Caesarea in Cappadocia through these years. The judgments formed about this great doctor in his lifetime show us vividly the extreme confusion which prevailed. He was accused by one party of being a follower of Apollinaris, and lost in consequence some of the sees over which he was metropolitan. He was accused by the monks in his friend Gregory's diocese of favouring the semi-Arians. He was accused by the Neocaesareans of inclining towards Arianism. And he was treated with suspicion and coldness by Pope Damasus.

17. About A.D. 360, St. Hilary says: "I am not speaking of things foreign to my knowledge; I am not writing about what I am ignorant of; I have heard and I have seen the shortcomings of persons who are present to me, not of laymen, but of Bishops. For, excepting the Bishop Eleusius and a few with him, for the most part the ten Asian provinces, within whose boundaries I am situate, are truly ignorant of God." It is observable, that even Eleusius, who is here spoken of as somewhat better than the rest, was a semi-Arian, according to Socrates, and even a persecutor of Catholics at Constantinople; and, according to Sozomen, one of those who urged Pope Liberius to give up the Nicene formula of the "Consubstantial." By the ten Asian provinces is meant the east and south provinces of Asia

Minor, pretty nearly as cut off by a line passing from Cyzicus to Seleucia through Synnada.

18. A.D. 360. St. Gregory Nazianzen says, about this date: "Surely the pastors have done foolishly; for, excepting a very few, who, either on account of their insignificance were passed over, or who by reason of their virtue resisted, and who were to be left as a seed and root for the springing up again and revival of Israel by the influences of the Spirit, all temporised, only differing from each other in this, that some succumbed earlier, and others later; some were foremost champions and leaders in the impiety, and others joined the second rank of the battle, being overcome by fear, or by interest, or by flattery, or, what was the most excusable, by their own ignorance." *Orat.* xxi. 24.

19. A.D. 363. About this time, St. Jerome says: "Nearly all the churches in the whole world, under the pretence of peace and the emperor, are polluted with the communion of the Arians." *Chron.* Of the same date, that is, upon the council of Ariminum, are his famous words, "Ingemuit totus orbis et se esse Arianum miratus est." *In Lucif.* That is, the Catholics of Christendom were surprised indeed to find that their rulers had made Arians of them.

20. A.D. 364. And St. Hilary: "Up to this date, the only cause why Christ's people is not murdered by the priests of Anti-christ, with this deceit of impiety, is, that they take the words which the heretics use, to denote the faith which they themselves hold. Sanctiores aures plebis quàm corda sunt sacerdotum." *In Aux.* 6.

21. St. Hilary speaks of the series of ecclesiastical councils of the time in the following well-known passage: "It is most dangerous to us, and it is lamentable, that there are at present as many creeds as there are sentiments, and as many doctrines among us as dispositions, while we write creeds and explain them according to our fancy. Since the

Nicene council, we have done nothing but write the creed.
While we fight about words, inquire about novelties, take
advantage of ambiguities, criticise authors, fight on party
questions, have difficulties in agreeing, and prepare to anathematise each other, there is scarce a man who belongs
to Christ. Take, for instance, last year's creed, what altera-
tion is there not in it already? First, we have the creed,
which bids us not to use the Nicene 'consubstantial;' then
comes another, which decrees and preaches it; next, the
third, excuses the word 'substance,' as adopted by the
fathers in their simplicity; lastly, the fourth, instead of
excusing, condemns. We impose creeds by the year or by
the month, we change our minds about our own imposition of them, then we prohibit our changes, then we
anathematise our prohibitions. Thus, we either condemn
others in our own persons, or ourselves in the instance of
others, and while we bite and devour one another, are like
to be consumed one of another."

22. A.D. 382. St. Gregory writes: "If I must speak the
truth, I feel disposed to shun every conference of Bishops;
for never saw I synod brought to a happy issue, and
remedying, and not rather aggravating, existing evils. For
rivalry and ambition are stronger than reason,—do not
think me extravagant for saying so,—and a mediator is
more likely to incur some imputation himself than to clear
up the imputations which others lie under." *Ep.* 129. It
must ever be kept in mind that a passage like this only relates, and is here quoted as only relating, to that miserable
time of which it is spoken. Nothing more can be argued
from it that that the "Ecclesia docens" is not at every time
the active instrument of the Church's infallibility.

II. Now we come secondly to the proofs of the fidelity
of the laity, and the effectiveness of that fidelity, during
that domination of imperial heresy to which the foregoing

passages have related. I have abridged the extracts which
follow, but not, I hope, to the injury of their sense.

1. ALEXANDRIA. "We suppose," says Athanasius, "you
are not ignorant what outrages they (the Arian Bishops)
committed at Alexandria, for they are reported everywhere. They attacked the *holy virgins and brethren* with
naked swords; they beat with scourges their persons,
esteemed honourable in God's sight, so that their feet were
lamed by the stripes, whose souls were whole and sound in
purity and all good works." Athan. *Op. c. Arian.* 15.

"Accordingly Constantius writes letters, and com-
mences *a persecution against all*. Gathering together a
multitude of herdsmen and shepherds, and dissolute
youths belonging to the town, armed with swords and
clubs, they attacked in a body *the Church* of Quirinus: and
some they slew, *some* they trampled under foot, *others*
they beat with stripes and cast into prison or banished.
They hauled away many *women* also, and dragged them
openly into the court, and insulted them, dragging them
by the hair. *Some* they proscribed; from *some* they took
away their bread, for no other reason but that they might
be induced to join the Arians, and receive Gregory (the
Arian Bishop), who had been sent by the Emperor."
Athan. *Hist. Arian.* 10.

"On the week that succeeded the holy Pentecost, when
the *people,* after their fast, had gone out to the cemetery
to pray, because that *all* refused communion with George
(the Arian Bishop), the commander, Sebastian, straight-
way with a multitude of soldiers proceeded to *attack the
people,* though it was the Lord's day; and finding a few
praying, (for the greater part had already retired on
account of the lateness of the hour,) having lighted a pile,
he placed certain *virgins* near the fire, and endeavoured to

force them to say that they were of the Arian faith. And having seized on *forty men,* he cut some fresh twigs of the palm-tree, with the thorns upon them, and scourged them on the back so severely that some of them were for a long time under medical treatment, on account of the thorns which had entered their flesh, and others, unable to bear up under their sufferings, died. All those whom they had taken, both the men and the virgins, they sent away into banishment to the great oasis. Moreover, they immediately banished out of Egypt and Libya the following Bishops (sixteen), and the presbyters, Hierax and Dioscorus: some of them died on the way, others in the place of their banishment. They caused also more than thirty Bishops to take to flight." *Apol. de Fug.* 7.

2. EGYPT. "The Emperor Valens having issued an edict commanding that the orthodox should be expelled both from Alexandria and the rest of Egypt, *depopulation and ruin to an immense extent immediately followed; some* were dragged before the tribunals, others cast into prison, and many tortured in various ways; all sorts of punishment being inflicted upon persons who aimed only at peace and quiet." Socr. *Hist.* iv. 24.

3. THE MONKS OF EGYPT. "*Antony left the solitude* of the desert to go about every part of the city (Alexandria), warning the inhabitants that the Arians were opposing the truth, and that the doctrines of the Apostles were preached only by Athanasius." Theod. *Hist.* iv. 27.

"Lucius, the Arian, with a considerable body of troops, proceeded to the *monasteries* of Egypt, where he in person assailed the assemblage of holy men with greater fury than the ruthless soldiery. When these excellent persons remained unmoved by all the violence, in despair he advised the military chief to send the fathers of the monks, the

Egyptian Macarius and his namesake of Alexandria, into exile." Socr. iv. 24.

OF CONSTANTINOPLE. "*Isaac,* on seeing the emperor depart at the head of his army, exclaimed, 'You who have declared war against God cannot gain His aid. Cease from fighting against Him, and He will terminate the war. Restore the pastors to their flocks, and then you will obtain a bloodless victory." (Theod., iv.)

OF SYRIA, &c. "That these heretical doctrines (Apollinarian and Eunomian) did not finally become predominant is *mainly to be attributed to the zeal of the monks* of this period; for *all the monks* of Syria, Cappadocia, and the neighbouring provinces *were sincerely attached to the Nicene faith.* The same fate awaited them which had been experienced by the Arians; for they incurred the full weight of the popular odium and aversion, when it was observed that their sentiments were regarded with suspicion, by the monks." Sozom., vi, 27.

OF CAPPADOCIA. "Gregory, the father of Gregory Theologus, otherwise a most excellent man and a zealous defender of the true and Catholic religion, not being on his guard against the artifices of the Arians, such was his simplicity, received with kindness certain men who were contaminated with the poison, and subscribed an impious proposition of theirs. This moved the monks to such indignation, that they *withdrew forthwith from his communion,* and took with them, after their example, *a considerable part of his flock.*" Ed. Bened. *Monit. in Greg. Naz.* Orat. 6.

4. ANTIOCH. "Whereas he (the Bishop Leontius) took part in the blasphemy of Arius, he made a point of concealing this disease, partly *for fear of the multitude,* partly for the menaces of Constantius; so those who followed the apostolical dogmas gained from him neither patronage nor

ordination, but those who held Arianism were allowed the fullest liberty of speech, and were placed in the ranks of the sacred ministry. But Flavian and Diodorus, who had embraced the ascetical life, and maintained the apostolical dogmas, *openly withstood* Leontius's machinations against religious doctrine. They threatened that they would retire from the communion of his Church, and would go to the West, and reveal his intrigues. Though they were not as yet in the sacred ministry, but were *in the ranks of the laity,* night and day they used to excite all the people to zeal for religion. They were the first to divide the singers into two choirs, and to teach them to sing alternately the strains of David. They too, assembling the devout at the shrines of the martyrs, passed the whole night there in hymns to God. These things Leontius seeing, did not think it safe to hinder them, for he saw that *the multitude was especially well affected* towards those excellent persons. Nothing, however, could persuade Leontius to correct his wickedness. It follows, that among the clergy were many who were infected with the heresy: but *the mass of the people were champions of orthodoxy.*" Theodor. *Hist.* ii. 24.

5. EDESSA. "There is in that city a magnificent church, dedicated to St. Thomas the Apostle, wherein, on account of the sanctity of the place, religious assemblies are continually held. The Emperor Valens wished to inspect this edifice; when, having learned that *all who usually congregated there were opposed to the heresy* which he favoured, he is said to have struck the prefect with his own hand, because he had neglected to expel them hence. The prefect, to prevent the slaughter of *so great a number* of persons, privately warned them against resorting thither. But his admonitions and menaces were alike unheeded; for on the following day *they all crowded to the church.* When the

prefect was going towards it with a large military force, a poor woman, leading her own little child by the hand, hurried hastily by on her way to the church, breaking through the ranks of the soldiery. The prefect, irritated at this, ordered her to be brought to him, and thus addressed her: 'Wretched woman, whither are you running in so disorderly a manner?' She replied, 'To the same place that others are hastening.' 'Have you not heard,' said he, 'that the prefect is about to put to death all that shall be found there?' 'Yes,' said the woman, 'and therefore I hasten, that I may be found there.' 'And whither are you dragging that little child?' said the prefect. The woman answered, *'That he also may be vouchsafed the honor of martyrdom.'* The prefect went back and informed the emperor that *all were ready to die in behalf of their own faith;* and added that it would be preposterous to destroy so many persons at one time, and thus succeeded in restraining the emperor's wrath." Socr. iv. 18. "Thus was the Christian faith confessed by the *whole city* of Edessa." Sozom. vi. 18.

6. SAMOSATA. "The Arians having deprived this exemplary flock of their shepherd, elected in his place an individual with whom *none of the inhabitants of the city,* whether poor or rich, servants or mechanics, husbandmen or gardeners, men or women, young or old, would hold communion. *He was left quite alone;* no one even calling to see him, or exchanging a word with him. It is, however, said that his disposition was extremely gentle; and this is proved by what I am about to relate. One day, when he went to bathe in the public baths, the attendants closed the doors; but he ordered the doors to be thrown open, that the people might be admitted to bathe with himself. Perceiving that they remained in a standing posture before him, imagining that great deference towards himself was

the cause of this conduct, he arose and left the bath. *These people believed that the water had been contaminated by his heresy,* and ordered it to be let out and fresh water to be supplied. When he heard of this circumstance, he left the city, thinking that he ought no longer to remain in a place *where he was the object of public aversion and hatred.* Upon this retirement of Eunomius, Lucius was elected as his successor by the Arians. Some young persons were amusing themselves with playing at ball in the market-place; Lucius was passing by at the time, and the ball happened to fall beneath the feet of the ass on which he was mounted. *The youths uttered loud exclamations, believing that the ball was contaminated.* They lighted a fire, and hurled the ball through it, believing that by this process the ball would be purified. Although this was only a childish deed, and although it exhibits the remains of ancient superstition, yet it is *sufficient to show the odium which the Arian faction had incurred in this city.* Lucius was far from imitating the mildness of Eunomius, and he persuaded the heads of government to exile most of the clergy." Theodor. iv. 15.

7. OSRHOENE. "Arianism met with similar opposition at the same period in Osrhoene and Cappadocia. Basil, Bishop of Caesarea, and Gregory, Bishop of Nazianzus, were held in high admiration and esteem *throughout these regions.*" Sozom. vi. 21.

8. CAPPADOCIA. "Valens, in passing through Cappadocia, did all in his power to injure the orthodox, and to deliver up the churches to the Arians. He thought to accomplish his designs more easily on account of a dispute which was then pending between Basil and Eusebius, who governed the Church of Caesarea. This dissension had been the cause of Basil's departing to Pontus. *The people, and some of the most powerful and wisest men of the city,*

began to regard Eusebius with suspicion, and to meditate a secession from his communion. The emperor and the Arian Bishops regarded the absence of Basil, and the hatred of the people towards Eusebius, as circumstances that would tend greatly to the success of their designs. *But their expectations were utterly frustrated.* On the first intelligence of the intention of the emperor to pass through Cappadocia, Basil returned to Caesarea, where he effected a reconciliation with Eusebius. The projects of Valens were thus defeated, and he returned with his Bishops." Sozom. vi. 15.

9. PONTUS. "It is said that when Eulalius, Bishop of Amasia in Pontus, returned from exile, he found that his Church had passed into the hands of an Arian, and that *scarcely fifty inhabitants of the city* had submitted to the control of their new Bishop." Sozom. vii. 2.

10. ARMENIA. "That company of Arians, who came with Eustathius to Nicopolis, had promised that they would bring over this city to compliance with the commands of the imperial vicar. This city had great ecclesiastical importance, both because it was the metropolis of Armenia, and because it had been ennobled by the blood of martyrs, and governed hitherto by Bishops of great reputation, and thus, as Basil calls it, was the nurse of religion and the metropolis of sound doctrine. Fronto, one of the city presbyters, who had hitherto shown himself as a champion of the truth, through ambition gave himself up to the enemies of Christ, and purchased the bishopric of the Arians at the price of renouncing the Catholic faith. This wicked proceeding of Eustathius and the Arians brought a new glory instead of evil to the Nicopolitans, since it gave them an opportunity of defending the faith. Fronto, indeed, the Arians consecrated, *but there was a remarkable unanimity of clergy and people in rejecting him.*

Scarcely one or two clerks sided with him; on the contrary, he *became the execration of all Armenia." Vita S. Basil.,* Bened. pp. clvii, clviii.

11. NICOMEDIA. "Eighty pious clergy proceeded to Nicomedia, and there presented to the emperor a supplicatory petition complaining of the ill-usage to which they had been subjected. Valens, dissembling his displeasure in their presence, gave Modestus, the prefect, a secret order to apprehend these persons and put them to death. The prefect, *fearing that he should excite the populace to a seditious movement* against himself, if he attempted the public execution of so many, pretended to send them away into exile," &c. Socr. iv. 16.

12. ASIA MINOR. St. Basil says, about the year 372: "Religious people keep silence, but every blaspheming tongue is let loose. Sacred things are profaned; *those of the laity* who are sound in faith *avoid the places of worship* as schools of impiety, and raise their hands in solitude, with groans and tears, to the Lord in heaven." *Ep.* 92. Four years after he writes: "Matters have come to this pass; *the people have left their houses of prayer,* and assemble in deserts: a pitiable sight; *women and children, old men, and infirm,* wretchedly faring in the open air, amid the most profuse rains and snow-storms, and winds, and frosts of winter; and again in summer under a scorching sun. To this they submit, because they *will have no part in the wicked Arian leaven." Ep.* 242. Again: "Only one offence is now vigorously punished, an accurate observance of our fathers' traditions. For this cause the pious are driven from their countries, and transported into deserts. The *people are in lamentation,* in continual tears at home and abroad. There is a cry in the city, a cry in the country, in the roads, in the deserts. Joy and spiritual cheerfulness are no more; our feasts are turned into mourning; our

houses of prayer are shut up, our altars deprived of the spiritual worship." *Ep.* 243.

13-14. SCYTHIA. "There are in this country a great number of cities, of towns, and of fortresses. According to an ancient custom which still prevails, all the churches of the whole country are under the sway of one Bishop. Valens (the emperor) repaired to the church, and strove to gain over the Bishop to the heresy of Arius; but this latter manfully opposed his arguments, and, after a courageous defence of the Nicene doctrines, quitted the emperor, and proceeded to another church, *whither he was followed by the people. Valens was extremely offended at being left alone* in a church with his attendants, and, in resentment, condemned Vetranio (the Bishop) to banishment. Not long after, however, he recalled him, because, I believe, *he apprehended an insurrection.*" Sozom. vi. 21.

15. CONSTANTINOPLE. "Those who acknowledged the doctrine of consubstantiality were not only expelled from the churches, but also from the cities. But although expulsion at first satisfied them (the Arians), they soon proceeded to the worse extremity of inducing compulsory communion with them, caring little for such a desecration of the churches. They resorted to all kinds of scourgings, a variety of tortures, and confiscation of property. Many were punished with exile, some died under the torture, and others were put to death while being driven from their country. *These atrocities were exercised throughout all the eastern cities,* but especially at Constantinople." Socr. ii. 27.

16. ILLYRIA. "The parents of Theodosius were Christians, and were attached to the Nicene doctrine, hence he took pleasure in the ministration of Ascholius (Bishop of Thessalonica). He also rejoiced at finding that the *Arian heresy had not been received in Illyria.*" Sozom. vii. 4.

17. NEIGHBORHOOD OF MACEDONIA. "Theodosius inquired concerning the religious sentiments which were prevalent in the other provinces, and ascertained that, as far as Macedonia, *one form of belief was universally predominant,*" &c. Ibid.

18. ROME. "With respect to doctrine no dissension arose either at Rome or in any other of the Western Churches. *The people unanimously adhered to the form of belief established at Nicaea.*" Sozom. vi. 23.

"Liberius, returning to Rome, found the *mind of the mass of men alienated from him,* because he had so shamefully yielded to Constantius. And thus it came to pass, that those persons who had hitherto kept aloof from Felix (the rival Pope), and had avoided his communion in favor of Liberius, on hearing what had happened, *left him for Felix,* who raised the Catholic standard. Baron. ann. 357, 56. He tells us besides (57), that the people would not even go to the public baths, lest they should bathe with the party of Liberius.

19. MILAN. "At the council of Milan, Eusebius of Vercellae, when it was proposed to draw up a declaration against Athanasius, said that the council ought first to be sure of the faith of the Bishops attending it, for he had found out that some of them were polluted with heresy. Accordingly he brought before the Fathers the Nicene creed, and said he was willing to comply with all their demands, after they had subscribed that confession. Dionysius, Bishop of Milan, at once took up the paper and began to write his assent; but Valens (the Arian) violently pulled pen and paper out of his hands, crying out that such a course of proceeding was impossible. Whereupon, after much tumult, *the question came before the people, and great was the distress of all of them;* the faith of the Church was attacked by the Bishops. *They then, dreading*

the judgment of the people, transfer their meeting from the church to the imperial palace." Hilar. *ad Const.* i., 8.

"As the feast of Easter approached, the empress sent to St. Ambrose to ask a church of him, where the Arians who attended her might meet together. He replied, that a Bishop could not give up the temple of God. The pretorian prefect came into the church, where St. Ambrose was *attended by the people,* and endeavoured to persuade him to yield up at least the Portian Basilica. *The people were clamorous against the proposal;* and the prefect retired to report how matters stood to the emperor. The Sunday following, St. Ambrose was explaining the creed, when he was informed that the officers were hanging up the imperial hangings in the Portian Basilica, and that upon this news the people were repairing thither. While he was offering up the holy sacrifice, a second message came that the *people had seized an Arian priest* as he was passing through the street. He despatched a number of his clergy to the spot to *rescue the Arian from his danger.* The court looked on this resistance of the people as seditious, and immediately laid considerable fines upon *the whole body of the tradesmen* of the city. Several were thrown into prison. In three days' time these tradesmen were fined two hundred pounds weight of gold, and they said *that they were ready to give as much again, on condition that they might retain their faith.* The prisons were filled with tradesmen: *all the officers of the household,* secretaries, agents of the emperor, and dependent officers who served under various counts, were kept within doors, and were forbidden to appear in public under pretence that they should bear no part in the sedition. *Men of higher rank* were menaced with severe consequences, unless the Basilica were surrendered. . . .

"Next morning the Basilica was surrounded by soldiers;

but it was reported, that *these soldiers had sent to the emperor to tell him* that if he wished to come abroad he might, and that they would attend him, if he was going to the assembly of the Catholics; otherwise, that they *would go to that which would be held by St. Ambrose.* Indeed, the *soldiers were all Catholics,* as well as the citizens of Milan; there were no heretics there, except a few officers of the emperor and some Goths. . . .

"St. Ambrose was continuing his discourse when he was told that the emperor had withdrawn the soldiers from the Basilica, and that he had restored to the tradesmen the fines which he had exacted from them. *This news gave joy to the people,* who expressed their delight with applauses and thanksgivings; *the soldiers themselves were eager to bring the news,* throwing themselves on the altars, and kissing them in token of peace." Fleury's *Hist.* xviii. 41, 42, Oxf. trans.

20. CHRISTENDOM GENERALLY. St. Hilary to Constantius: "Not only in words, but in tears, we beseech you to save the Catholic Churches from any longer continuance of these most grievous injuries, and of their present intolerable persecutions and insults, which moreover they are enduring, which is monstrous, from our brethren. Surely your clemency should listen to the *voice of those who cry out so loudly,* 'I am a Catholic, I have no wish to be a heretic.' It should seem equitable to your sanctity, most glorious Augustus, that they who fear the Lord God and His judgment should not be polluted and contaminated with execrable blasphemies, but *should have liberty to follow those Bishops and prelates* who observe inviolate the laws of charity, and who desire a perpetual and sincere peace. It is impossible, it is unreasonable, to mix true and false, to confuse light and darkness, and bring into a union of whatever kind, night and day. *Give permission to the*

populations to hear the teaching of the pastors whom they have wished, whom they fixed on, whom they have chosen, to attend their celebration of the divine mysteries, to offer prayers through them for your safety and prosperity." *ad Const.* i. 2.

Now I know quite well what will be said to so elaborate a collection of instances as I have been making. The "lector benevolus" will quote against me the words of Cicero, "Utitur in re non dubiâ testibus non necessariis." This is sure to befall a man when he directs the attention of a friend to any truth which hitherto he has thought little of. At first, he seems to be hazarding a paradox, and at length to be committing a truism. The hearer is first of all startled, and then disappointed; he ends by asking, "Is this all?" It is a curious phenomenon in the philosophy of the human mind, that we often do not know whether we hold a point or not, though we hold it; but when our attention is once drawn to it, then forthwith we find it so much part of ourselves, that we cannot recollect when we began to hold it, and we conclude (with truth), and we declare, that it has always been our belief. Now it strikes me as worth noticing, that, though Father Perrone is so clear upon the point of doctrine which I have been urging in 1847, yet in 1842, which is the date of my own copy of his *Praelectiones,* he has not given the *consensus fidelium* any distinct place in his *Loci Theologici,* though he has given "heretici" a place there. Among the *Media Traditionis,* he enumerates the *magisterium* of the Church, the Acts of the Martyrs, the Liturgy, usages and rites of worship, the Fathers, heretics, Church history; but not a word, that I can find, directly and separately, about the *sensus fidelium.* This is the more remarkable, because, speaking of the *Acta Martyrum,* he gives a reason for the force of the testimony of the martyrs which belongs quite as fully to the faithful generally; viz. that, as not being theologians, they can only repeat that objective truth, which, on the other hand, Fathers and theologians do but present subjectively, and thereby coloured with their own mental peculiarities. "We learn from them," he says, "what was the traditionary doctrine in both domestic and public assemblies of the Church, without any admixture of private and (so to say) subjective explanation, such as at times creates a difficulty in ascertaining the real meaning of the Fathers; and so much the more, because many of them were either women or ordinary and untaught laymen, who brought out and avowed just what they believed in a straightforward inartificial way." May we not conjecture that the argument from the Consent of the Faithful was but dimly written among the *Loci* on the tablets of his intellect, till the necessities, or rather the requirements, of the contemplated definition of the Immaculate Conception brought the argument before him with great force? Yet who will therefore for an instant suppose that he did not always hold it? Perhaps I have overlooked some passage of his treatises and am in consequence interpreting his course of thought wrongly; but, at any rate, what I seem to see in him, is what actually does occur from time to time in myself and others. A man holds an opinion or a truth, yet without holding it with a simple consciousness and a direct recognition; and thus, though he had never denied, he has never gone so far as to profess it.

As to the particular doctrine of which I have here been directing my view, and the passage in history by which I have been illustrating it, I am not supposing that such times as the Arian will ever come again. As to the present, certainly, if there ever was an age which might dispense

with the testimony of the faithful, and leave the maintenance of the truth to the pastors of the Church, it is the
age in which we live. Never was the Episcopate of Christendom so devoted to the Holy See, so religious, so earnest
in the discharge of its special duties, so little disposed to
innovate, so superior to the temptation of theological
sophistry. And perhaps this is the reason why the "consensus fidelium" has, in the minds of many, fallen into the
background. Yet each constituent portion of the Church
has its proper functions, and no portion can safely be
neglected. Though the laity be but the reflection or echo
of the clergy in matters of faith, yet there is something
in the "pastorum et fidelium *conspiratio*," which is not in
the pastors alone. The history of the definition of the
Immaculate Conception shows us this; and it will be one
among the blessings which the Holy Mother, who is the
subject of it, will gain for us, in repayment of the definition,
that by that very definition we are all reminded of the part
which the laity have had in the preliminaries of its promul-
gation. Pope Pius has given us a pattern, in his manner
of defining, of the duty of considering the sentiments of
the laity upon a point of tradition, in spite of whatever
fullness of evidence the Bishops had already thrown upon
it.

In most cases when a definition is contemplated, the
laity will have a testimony to give, but if ever there be
an instance when they ought to be consulted, it is in the
case of doctrines which bear directly upon devotional
sentiments. Such is the Immaculate Conception, of which
the *Rambler* was speaking in the sentence which has
occasioned these remarks. The faithful people have ever
a special function in regard to those doctrinal truths which
relate to the Objects of worship. Hence it is, that, while
the Councils of the fourth century were traitors to our

Lord's divinity, the laity vehemently protested against its impugners. Hence it is, that, in a later age, when the learned Benedictines of Germany and France were perplexed in their enunciation of the doctrine of the Real Presence, Paschasius was supported by the faithful in his maintenance of it. The saints, again, are the object of a religious *cultus;* and therefore it was the faithful, again, who urged on the Holy See, in the time of John XXII., to declare their beatitude in heaven, though so many Fathers spoke variously. And the Blessed Virgin is preeminently an object of devotion; and therefore it is, I repeat, that though Bishops had already spoken in favour of her absolute sinlessness, the Pope was not content without knowing the feelings of the faithful.

Father Dalgairns gives us another case in point; and with his words I conclude: "While devotion in the shape of a dogma issues from the high places of the Church, in the shape of devotion . . . it starts from below. . . . Place yourselves, in imagination, in a vast city of the East in the fifth century. Ephesus, the capital of Asia Minor, is all in commotion; for a council is to be held there, and Bishops are flocking in from all parts of the world. There is anxiety painted on every face; so that you may easily see that the question is one of general interest. . . . Ask the very children in the streets what is the matter; they will tell you that wicked men are coming to make out that their own mother is not the Mother of God. And so, during a livelong day of June, they crowd around the gates of the old cathedral-church of St. Mary and watch with anxious faces each Bishop as he goes in. Well might they be anxious for it is well known that Nestorius has won the court over to his side. It was only the other day that he entered the town, with banners displayed and trumpets sounding, surrounded by the glittering files of the em-

peror's body-guard, with Count Candidianus, their general
and his own partisan, at their head. Besides which, it is
known for certain, that at least eighty-four Bishops are
ready to vote with him; and who knows how many more?
He is himself the patriarch of Constantinople, the rival
of Rome, the imperial city of the East; and then John of
Antioch is hourly expected with his quota of votes; and he,
the patriarch of the see next in influence to that of Nestorius, is, if not a heretic, at least of that wretched party
which, in ecclesiastical disputes, ever hovers between the
two camps of the devil and of God. The day wears on,
and still nothing issues from the church; it proves, at
least, that there is a difference of opinion; and as the
shades of evening close around them, the weary watchers
grow more anxious still. At length the great gates of the
Basilica are thrown open; and oh, what a cry of joy bursts
from the assembled crowd, as it is announced to them that
Mary has been proclaimed to be, what every one with a
Catholic heart knew that she was before, the Mother
of God! . . . Men, women, and children, the noble and
the low-born, the stately matron and the modest maiden,
all crowd round the Bishops with acclamations. They
will not leave them; they accompany them to their homes
with a long procession of lighted torches; they burn in-
cense before them, after the eastern fashion, to do them
honour. There was but little sleep in Ephesus that night;
for very joy they remained awake; the whole town was
one blaze of light, for each window was illuminated." [1]

My own drift is somewhat different from that which
has dictated this glowing description; but the substance
of the argument of each of us is one and the same. I think
certainly that the *Ecclesia docens* is more happy when

[1] Sacred Heart

she has such enthusiastic partisans about her as are here
represented, than when she cuts off the faithful from the
study of her divine doctrines and the sympathy of her
divine contemplations, and requires from them a *fides
implicita* in her word, which in the educated classes will
terminate in indifference, and in the poorer in superstition.

5

The 'Arians' Note

In Note V appended to his third edition of "The Arians of the Fourth Century" (1873), Newman published a summary of his famous *"Rambler"* article. He made certain modifications, notably concerning the passage in which he had written that "there was a temporary *suspense* of the functions of the Ecclesia docens." Newman also suppressed the allusions to the persecutions of St. Basil, and the claim that Basil "was treated with suspicion and coldness by Pope Damasus." He also eliminated St. Hilary's accusation that the ears of the laity were holier than the hearts of the Clergy: *Sanctiores aures plebis quam corda sunt sacerdotum.* The following is Newman's note:

The episcopate, whose action was so prompt and concordant at Nicaea on the rise of Arianism, did not, as a class or order of men, play a good part in the troubles consequent upon the Council; and the laity did. The Catholic people, in the length and breadth of Christendom, were the obstinate champions of Catholic truth, and the Bishops were not. Of course there were great and illustrious exceptions; first, Athanasius, Hilary, the

Latin Eusebius, and Phoebadius; and after them, Basil, the two Gregories, and Ambrose; there are others, too, who suffered, if they did nothing else, as Eustathius, Paulus, Paulinus, and Dionysius; and the Egyptian bishops, whose weight was small in the Church in proportion to the great power of their Patriarch. And, on the other hand, as I shall say presently, there were exceptions to the Christian heroism of the laity, especially in some of the great towns. And again, in speaking of the laity, I speak inclusively of their parish-priests (so to call them), at least in many places; but on the whole, taking a wide view of the history, we are obliged to say that the governing body of the Church came short, and the governed were pre-eminent in faith, zeal, courage, and constancy.

This is a very remarkable fact: but there is a moral in it. Perhaps it was permitted, in order to impress upon the Church at that very time passing out of her state of persecution to her long temporal ascendancy, the great evangelical lesson, that, not the wise and powerful, but the obscure, the unlearned, and the weak constitute her real strength. It was mainly by the faithful people that Paganism was overthrown; it was by the faithful people, under the lead of Athanasius and the Egyptian bishops, and in some places supported by their Bishops or priests, that the worst of heresies was withstood and stamped out of the sacred territory.

Newman then gives the second part of his diptych, the part which shows in connection with the indecision of the Bishops, the fidelity of the laity. He continues as follows:

Coming to the opposite side of the contrast, I observe that there were great efforts made on the part of the Arians to render their heresy popular. Arius himself, according to the Arian Philostorgius, "wrote songs for the sea, and for the mill, and for the road, and then set them to suitable music." Hist. ii. 2. Alexander speaks of the "running about" of the Arian women, Theod. Hist. i. 4, and of the buffoonery of their men, Socrates says that "in the Imperial court, the officers of the bed-chamber held disputes with the women, and in the city, in every house, there was a war of dialectics," ii. 2. Especially at Constantinople there were as Gregory says, "of Jezebels as thick a crop as of hemlock in a field," Orat. 35, 3; and he himself suffered from the popular violence there. At Alexandria the Arian women are described by Athanasius as "running up and down like Bacchanals and furies," and as "passing that day in grief on which they could do no harm." *Hist. Arian.* 59.

The controversy was introduced in ridicule into the heathen theatres, Euseb. v. Const. ii. 6. Socr. i. 6. "Men of yesterday," says Gregory Nyssen, "mere mechanics, off-hand dogmatists in theology, servants too and slaves that have been scourged, run-aways from servile work, and philosophical about things incomprehensible. Of such the city is full; its entrances, forums, squares, thorough-fares; the clothes-vendors, the money-lenders, the victu-allers. Ask about pence, and they will discuss the generate and ingenerate," etc., etc., tom. ii. p. 898. Socrates, too, says that the heresy "ravaged provinces and cities"; and Theodoret that, "quarrels took place in every city and village concerning the divine dogma, the people looking on, and taking sides." *Hist.* i. 6.

In spite of these attempts, however, on the part of the Arians, still, viewing Christendom as a whole, we shall find that the Catholic populations sided with Athanasius; and the fierce disputes above described evidenced the zeal of the orthodox rather than the strength of the heretical party.

Newman here repeats the texts we have already given in Chapter Four, and he continues as follows:

In drawing out this comparison between the conduct of the Catholic Bishops and that of their flocks during the Arian troubles, I must not be understood as intending any conclusion inconsistent with the infallibility of the Ecclesia docens, (that is, the Church when teaching) and with the claim of the Pope and the Bishops to constitute the Church in that aspect. I am led to give this caution, because, for the want of it, I was seriously misunderstood in some quarters on my first writing on the above subject in the *Rambler* Magazine of May, 1859. But on that occasion, I was writing simply historically, not doctrinally, and, while it is historically true, it is in no sense doctrinally false, that a Pope, as a private doctor, and much more Bishops, when not teaching formally, may err, as we find they did err in the fourth century. Pope Liberius might sign a Eusebian formula at Sirmium, and the mass of Bishops at Ariminum or elsewhere, and yet they might, in spite of this error, be infallible in their *ex cathedra* decisions.

The reason of my being misunderstood arose from two or three clauses or expressions which occurred in the course of my remarks, which I should not have used had I anticipated how they would be taken, and which I avail myself of this opportunity to explain and withdraw. First, I will quote the passage which bore a meaning which I certainly did not intend, and then I will note the phrases which seem to have given this meaning to it. It will be seen how little, when those phrases are withdrawn, the sense of the passage, as I intended it, is affected by the withdrawal. I said then:—

"It is not a little remarkable, that, though, historically speaking, the fourth century is the age of doctors, illustrated, as it is, by the Saints Athanasius, Hilary, the two Gregories, Basil, Chrysostom, Ambrose, Jerome, and Augustine, (and all those saints bishops also), except one, nevertheless in that very day the Divine tradition committed to the infallible Church was proclaimed and maintained far more by the faithful than by the Episcopate.

"Here of course I must explain:—in saying this then, undoubtedly I am not denying that the great body of the Bishops were in their internal belief orthodox; nor that there were numbers of clergy who stood by the laity and acted as their centres and guides; nor that the laity actually received their faith, in the first instance, from the Bishops and clergy; nor that some portions of the laity were ignorant, and other portions were at length corrupted by the Arian teachers, who got possession of the sees, and ordained an heretical clergy:—but I mean still, that in that time of immense confusion the divine dogma of our Lord's divinity was proclaimed, enforced, maintained, and (humanly speaking) preserved, far more by the 'Ecclesia docta' than by the 'Ecclesia docens'; that the body of the Episcopate was unfaithful to its commission, while the body of the laity was faithful to its baptism; that at one time the pope, at other times a patriarchal, metropolitan, or other great see, at other times general councils, said what they should not have said, or did what obscured and compromised revealed truth; while, on the other hand, it was the Christian people, who, under Providence, were the ecclesiastical strength of Athanasius, Hilary, Eusebius of Vercellae, and other great solitary confessors, who would have failed without them. . . .

"On the one hand, then, I say, that there was a temporary suspense of the functions of the 'Ecclesia docens.' The body of Bishops failed in their confession of the faith. They spoke variously, one against another; there was nothing, after Nicaea, of firm, unvarying, consistent testimony, for nearly sixty years. . . .

"We come secondly to the proofs of the fidelity of the laity, and the effectiveness of that fidelity, during that domination of Imperial heresy, to which the foregoing passages have related."

The three clauses which furnished matter of objection were these:—I said, (1) that "there was a temporary suspense of the functions of the 'Ecclesia docens' "; (2) that "the body of Bishops failed in their confession of the faith." (3) that "general councils, etc., said what they should not have said, or did what obscured and compromised revealed truth."

(1) That "there was a temporary *suspense* of the functions of the Ecclesia docens" is not true, if by saying so is meant that the Council of Nicaea held in 325 did not sufficiently define and promulgate for all times and all places the dogma of our Lord's divinity, and that the notoriety of that Council and the voices of its great supporters and maintainers, as Athanasius, Hilary, etc., did not bring home the dogma to the intelligence of the faithful in all parts of Christendom. But what I meant by "suspense" (I did not say "suspension," purposely) was only this, that there was no authoritative utterance of the Church's infallible voice in matter of fact between the Nicene Council, A.D. 325, and the Council of Constantinople, A.D. 381, or, in the words which I actually used, "there was nothing after Nicaea of firm, unvarying, consistent testimony for nearly sixty years." As writing be-

fore the Vatican Definition of 1870, I did not lay stress upon the Roman Councils under Popes Julius and Damasus.[1]

(2) That "the *body* of Bishops failed in their confession of the faith," p. 17. Here, if the word "body" is used in the sense of the Latin "corpus," as "corpus" is used in theological treatises, and as it doubtless would be translated for the benefit of readers ignorant of the English language, certainly this would be a heretical statement. But I meant nothing of the kind. I used it in the vague, familiar, genuine sense of which Johnson gives instances in his dictionary as meaning "the great preponderance," or, "the mass" of Bishops, viewing them in the main or the gross, as a *cumulus* of individuals. Thus Hooker says, "Life and death have divided between them the whole body of mankind"; Clarendon, after speaking of the van of the king's army says, "in the body was the king and

1 A distinguished theologian infers from my words that I deny that "the Church is in every time the activum instrumentum docendi." But I do not admit the fairness of this inference. Distinguo: activum instrumentum docendi virtuale, C. Actuale, N. The Ecumenical Council of 325 was an effective authority in 341, 351, and 359, though at those dates the Arians were in the seats of teaching. Fr. Perrone   agrees with me. (1). He reckons the "fidelium sensus" among the "instrumenta traditionis." (*Immac. Concept.* p. 139). (2). He contemplates, nay he instances, the case in which the "sensus fidelium" supplies, as the "instrumentum," the absence of the other instruments, the *magisterium* of the Church, as exercised at Nicaea, being always supposed. One of his instances is that of the dogma de visione Dei beatifica. He says: "Certe quidem in Ecclesia non deerat quoad hunc fidei articulum divina traditio; alioquin, nunquam is definiri potuisset: verum non omnibus illa erat comperta: divina eloquia haud satis in re sunt conspicua; Patres, ut vidimus, in varias abierunt sententias; liturgiae ipsae non modicam prae se ferunt difficultatem. His omnibus succurrit juge Ecclesiae magisterium; communis praeterea fidelium sensus." p. 148.

the prince": and Addison speaks of "navigable rivers, which ran up into the body of Italy." In this sense it is true historically that the body of Bishops failed in their confession. Tillemont, quoting from St. Gregory Nazianzen, says, "La souscription (Arienne) était une des dispositions necessaires pour entrer et pour se conserver dans l'episcopat. L'encre était toujours toute prête, et l'accusateur aussi. Ceux qui avaient paru invincibles jusques alors, céderent à cette tempête. Si leur esprit ne tomba pas dans l'heresie, leur main néanmoins y consentit. . . . Peu d'Evêques s'exemterent de ce malheur, n'y ayant eu que ceux que leur propre bassesse faisait negliger, ou que leur vertu fit resister genereusement, et que Dieu conserva afin qu'il restât encore quelque semence et quelque racine pour faire refleurir Israel." T. vi. p. 499. In St. Gregory's own words *Plēn olígon ágan, pántes tou kaizou gegónasi tosouton allēlōn dienegkóntes, oson toùs mèn próteron, toùs dè ústeron touto pathein.*

(3) That "*general* councils said what they should not have said, and did what obscured and compromised revealed truth." Here again the question to be determined is what is meant by the word "general." If I meant by "general" ecumenical, I should have spoken as no Catholic can speak; but ecumenical Councils there were none between 325 and 381, and so I could not be referring to any; and in matter of fact I used the word "general" in *contrast* to "ecumenical," as I had used it in Tract No. 90, and as Bellarmine uses the word. He makes a fourfold division of "general Councils," viz., those which are approbata; reprobata; partim confirmata, partim reprobata; and nec manifeste probata nec manifeste reprobata. Among the "reprobata" he placed the Arian Councils. They were quite large enough to be called "generalia"; the twin

Councils of Seleucia and Ariminum numbering as many as 540 Bishops. When I spoke then of "general councils compromising revealed truth," I spoke of the Arian or Eusebian Councils, not of the Catholic.

I hope this is enough to observe on this subject.

PERSPECTIVES

6

Layman, Priest, Prophet

In this chapter, the reader will find some jottings on the still inadequately known person—the layman. These jottings have no order than the order of love, and love, as Pascal says, digresses. . . .

Philosophy of the Priest and the Prophet

Under the Old Law, the priest was not the prophet, nor was the prophet the priest. It was the priest's duty to perform the rites and sacrifices: he offered up the victims, he watched over the Temple. He was the intermediary between man and God. Here, the function was more important than the person. It was, of course, desirable that the levite or priest should be personally holy, but what was especially demanded of him was that he should carry out the liturgy according to the Mosaic precepts, that the sacrifice might be agreeable and acceptable to God.

The prophet is the man of God: *ish Eloim.* He may be a priest, but in most cases he is what we should call a layman, and sometimes of a low social level—a poor shepherd, for example. There are even prophetesses, such as Debora. The prophet receives his investiture from the Spirit, either directly or through another prophet who casts his mantle upon the new prophet. It was thus that Elias consecrated Eliseus. The prophet's task is to preach the word of God fearlessly, to recall all ranks of the nation to uprightness of life, to maintain the Tradition and to develop it, to restore the spirit of the law when the letter tends to kill its true meaning, or at least to interpret the law according to the Spirit. The prophets were not only seers, divines, even mystics; they were also the first teachers of the universal religion and of worship in spirit and in truth. They were the prototypes of our saints, our evangelists, sometimes of our martyrs. The Precursor was the greatest of them, for he pointed to Him Whom the prophets were imitating without expressly knowing that they were doing so, and Whom they announced in an obscure manner. Jesus Himself appeared in the condition of a prophet. He was neither a priest nor a levite, but a "layman" and a prophet—*vir propheta* as the disciples on the way to Emmaus described Him.

These distinctions are a great help towards our understanding the new Priesthood. The priest of the New Law is both priest and prophet.

He is a priest because the religion of Christ is a sacramental and social religion, in which no one comes to the Father but by the Son, and no one comes to the Son except through His representatives and their successors. Grace descends through the visible Church, and the Church is primarily the Apostles and their successors, the Bishops and priests. When they have been duly ordained and have received from apostolic authority the right to govern souls, only then are they the official and necessary intermediaries between the people and God. The priest administers the Sacraments; he receives into and reconciles with the Church; he breaks the Bread which is the Body of Christ. Without him, we should be without visible and sure means of going to the invisible Christ, without the Sacraments, without the Mass, without the Church.

But if the priest were merely a priest—in other words,

if he confined himself to baptizing, absolving, celebrating Mass, burying the dead—there would be every chance that religion would languish. It would no longer be other than a religion of rites, for which the people would quickly lose their respect and love. Of course, the rite carried out in due form and without a spirit of apostolate is much preferable to the complete absence of sacraments and the religion of the Only Word. For the rite, simply from the human point of view, is an action which contains more than it signifies; and, from God's point of view, the rite bears with it grace. And yet, clergy who would confine themselves to rites and to sacred gestures would not be the clergy whom Christ willed and established.

Following the traditions of the prophets, the priest of the New Law should, therefore, be a man of God as well as being the instrument of *the new and eternal Alliance.* He should preach by word and by example. His role is not completed when he has administered Baptism, celebrated Mass, recited his Breviary. In season and out of season, *he should go out to teach,* to evangelize, according to his strength and his capacities; he should bear the Word to the people, and adapt its expression to their understanding; he should explain the rites to them, and teach them how to pray; he should instruct them to understand that the Sacraments are directly connected with Christ, so that they do not come to regard them as simple practices of piety. He should increase his flock, which is the only way to preserve it; he should gather apostles around him, which is the only way to guard the fire of his own zeal, for zeal conserves itself only by self-propagation.

That, at least, is the ideal situation. In practice, however, it seems that *the prophetic element* and *the sacerdotal element* sometimes unfortunately clash with one another. In the primitive Church, there were the prophets, and, as we know from the *Acts* and from St. Paul, they were active; but they were in submision to the Apostle, to "the Bishops." It seems that the Apostolic authority and, later, the presbyteral and episcopal authority were sometimes distrustful of the prophets.

This is easy to understand. The prophet derived his inspiration from God, and was his own justification; his visible and sometimes spectacular works were the proof of his claim. His perfection and sometimes his strange mode of life attracted the respect of the people, who saw in him the evidence of a participation in the Spirit. The Church was obliged to fight against prophetism to the extent to which prophetism endangered its constitution, as when the prophet, not content with expressing the Spirit, behaved as a *pneumatophore,* on a level with the Hierarchy, claiming, for example, to remit sin. Gradually the idea clearly emerged that the value of the Sacraments does not depend on the personal qualities of the minister; without that distinction, indeed, no Church would have been possible. Can one ever say with full certainty that this or that priest is a man of God?

But in the very measure in which the *function* of the minister is affirmed on its own and apart from his *holiness,* the Church tends to become a sacred administration. This is the situation which gives birth to prophets within, and especially outside, the Church. Then the prophet is the "cathare," the Waldensian, the one who bases his message on the display of a state of life more saintly than that of the official priest. And the Dominican or the Franciscan is, if I may so put it, the orthodox prophet, proving by his example that one can be penetrated with the Spirit *and* submissive to the Church. However, it is remarkable that, in general, prophetism goes to seed. First, the prophet regards himself as the bearer of the Spirit, then as entrusted with power, then as impeccable. He ends up in anarchy, pride, aberration. Having set out to reform ritualism, he gradually slides towards a worse error.

I am reminded of a movie I saw recently, called *Dieu a Besoin des Hommes*—which could have had as sub-title *Priest and Prophet*. It shows that these two old problems are still with us. I am concerned only with the message of the story, not with its details. We are given a drama which is the reverse of the more usual one of the priest who "secularizes" himself and loses his faith along with his vocation. Here, it is a layman who is turned into a prophet. The people have no church and no priest, and, hungry for religion, they look to this man to be pure, austere, merciful, self-oblating for all, the man to whom sinners can unburden their guilt. To all intents and purposes, they "ordain" him, for the *île de Sein* demands that their hero, Thomas, absolve them, and be their minister of salvation.

But there, precisely, is the condition to which prophetism can never attain. The comunity can help Thomas to become almost *a prophet;* it can never make him *a priest*. The people can give themselves a prophet, who will represent their noblest aspirations, on whom they will place their sins, demanding that he should be holy in their place. They cannot produce a priest, that is, a man empowered by God to forgive sins in His name, and to change bread into His Body. This constitutes the divine part, the office utterly dependent on an *ordination* which can come from God alone. The prophet, however powerful, ranks below the priest; and it appears that, however great men's desire for prophetism, the necessity for the priesthood is more important. A man condemned to death would have no desire to see a prophet walk into his cell; he would want a priest, who could give him the security of Absolution.

The reactions of the audience to this movie were more interesting to watch than the movie itself. It seemed to me that the audience were responding to their own two great aspirations as shown in the story: that towards a holiness emanating from themselves and from their communities, a naked holiness without vestments, without rites, almost without walled churches, and speaking their language; and that towards a holiness issuing from God alone, communicated to His minister in the form of powers which are absolute and which make it possible to be truly initiated, cleansed, nourished in God, reassured by God, reconciled to God. They need these two living sources.

What is peculiar to our epoch more than to any other—and this brings us to the question of lay spirituality—is that each of these forms appears in one of two different subjects. Certainly, the priest-prophet, such as the Curé of Ars, will always catch the imagination and enthusiasm of the people, but more and more it is admitted that beside the priest is the prophet, that is, the holy layman. And a "spirituality" is being sought for this layman. I do not think it necessary to seek far, for such a spirituality is immanent in the Bible, in the *Acts of the Apostles*, in the Pauline Epistles. It is the prophetic spirituality.

For many among the middle classes, the workers, the peasants, the priest is still only the ritualist with power to absolve, with authority in sacred matters. Often such, alas, is the priest as desertion by the masses in town and country has made him: solitary, ascetic, bitter, alone. But, beneath the clerical vestment, each perceives the fundamental element of the Catholic priesthood, the element which is also sensed under the necessary rite, but of which

he has no clear idea. This element is the priest's participation in the One Priesthood of the One Pontiff and of
the One Mediator.

I was saying just now that, *in the historic order,* Jesus
was a prophet, a layman sent to death by the high priest.
But, *in the real and fundamental order,* He is the sole
Sacrificer and the only Priest and Pontiff.

In the unity of His theandric being, we find the two
elements of which we spoke. Christ is at once Priest and
Prophet: *prophet according to the temporal historic order,
priest according to the eternal and ontological order.*

The priest, modeled on Christ, is, like Him, priest and
prophet, but priest first and essentially, as we see in the
contemplative Religious Orders where the priest has no
active prophetic character.

The prophet imitates Christ solely in His prophetic
aspect. Actively caught up in various communities, in
contact with men of all kinds, involved in events and circumstances, bearing witness by his words and by his example, he cannot have any strictly sacred function, for he
cannot participate in the priesthood except in an analogous
and mystical way.

There is, therefore, a complex priest-and-prophet structure which is perfect only in Christ, but which is variously
participated in by men throughout time according to the
needs of the Church.

What we mean by *the laity* today seems to be an
original development of Catholic prophetism. The layman
belongs to temporal communities, and he is not a member
of the clerical community, which is something apart.
He is not to seek to be some kind of lay deacon, some
sort of hidden "priest" or clerical "fifth columnist" in the
world. It seems to me that Father Congar has elucidated

these different aspects with a great deal of prudence, competence and wisdom.

Perhaps our age will prove, more than other ages have done, how important it is that the layman should *form a real part* of the communities to which he belongs: family, profession, nation, and tomorrow perhaps, internation. The layman is one with the people, comes from the people, and is representative of their hidden aspirations.

Here we come to a cardinal difficulty of the lay state in the Church of today, a difficulty destined perhaps to be even more acute in the Church of tomorrow. Too often, we are offered the model and ideal of what is called *the pious laity,* and on analysis this is found to signify simply the transposing and even, so to speak, the transliterating of the life of the cloister into the life of the world. The "pious layman" is easily recognizable by his way of dressing, of speaking,, of "edifying," of behaving, of praying, of living. Clearly, there is no question of such behavior, which is in a sense much too simple and very weakly efficacious in its irradiation, except in the case of absolute sanctity. This is how we must understand the paradox confided to us by Mauriac in his *Pierre d'Achoppement* that if he had to re-live his life, *exactly as it had occurred,* he would take as much care to hide his Christian faith as he had taken to display it. By this he means that he would, as it were, bury it in the soil of his life, that he would incarnate it in his daily pattern of living. The task for the "prophet" is to enter into communion with the natural community of which he is a member, to root himself unobtrusively there so that he grows to a spiritual maturity redolent of the soil from which he has sprung. It seems to me that, in our age, this should be the objective of the laity.

Aspects of the Spirituality proper to the Laity

I have often been struck by the peculiar clerical attitude regarding the layman as a kind of diminished cleric. He is given a religious habit, but a *reduced* one, like the old "scapulars." Abridged Breviaries, and so forth, are prepared for his use. I fully appreciate that all this is aimed at enabling him to share as much as possible in the ideal Christian life as realized in the Religious Orders. This is the purpose of the "Third Orders." But I have often asked myself whether, instead of proposing to the layman a spirituality adapted to his way of life by being diminished by a few degrees of excellence, it would not be better to consider the pattern of lay life in itself. If such a type of spirituality does exist, it has the advantage of not being superimposed, for it expresses the proper work of the Spirit in the lay heart. It would seem, however, that this lay spirituality (to use a short term for what we have in mind) has not yet achieved an adequate expression. One finds it here and there, in a scattered way. One breathes it, for instance, in the spirit of St. Francis de Sales, or better still in the spirit of St. Theresa of Lisieux. It makes a spectacular appearance in St. Joan of Arc, but this saint is remote from us because of her era and her unusual history. Some years ago, in articles published in the *Revue des Jeunes,* Father Sertillanges made a splendid effort, in the spirit of St. Thomas Aquinas, to define this spirituality of daily life which has inspired his two splendid books *Le Travail Intellectuel* (English translation: "The Intellectual Life"—Mercier) and *Notre Vie.*

I see what is lacking, in this connection, to the Christian layman. To begin with the most obvious element, but one which is symbolical here, he has no "habit" in the religious sense. When Mustapha Kemal issued an order that Nuns should wear lay dress, there was consternation among the French "Sisters of Charity" in Turkey. The Superior of the Congregation of the Mission, Father Souvay, urged them to conform, on the grounds that the "cornette," the famous "bonnet," was not an essential element of their Charity or their exercise of Charity. But the Sisters could have replied that their dress was more than a symbol; for the bonnet is their vocation exteriorized, the virginal ideal made visible to others and to themselves, a kind of cloister accompanying them wherever they go. Barrès called the clerical soutane "the uniform of high moral preoccupations." Even when the priest wears lay dress, I think he should be distinguished by the addition of some insignia (by the Cross, for instance) in order that all may see that he is a priest. But the layman has no such badge or sign, for he must be like everyone else. The woman, especially, will follow the general fashion, dress according to the season, use "make-up" like the average of her sex. Similarly, the working man wears overalls. The lay ideal is here the opposite to that of the priest or the Religious. For reasons of apostolate, the latter may dress as a layman, but this does not alter the fact that his proper office is to represent the *sacred* among men. And the Religious habit symbolizes the mystery: it is the visible sign of the splendor of his calling.

What I have said about dress applies also to what is known in Religious Orders as "the Rule." One cannot require the layman to have a "rule" in this sense.

Consider, for example, morning rising. In our large towns, the layman's activities apart from his "job" must usually be fitted in after the evening meal—that is, between nine o'clock and midnight. How then could he be expected to rise at a very early hour, if he is to conserve his needed energy?

The layman who is of the professional class must conform to the social pattern of that class. He cannot retreat into "a Rule," constantly refusing "invitations to go out," or he can do so only at the cost of being considered an eccentric and of giving the impression that he is "a Religious living in the world." Indeed, the latter phrase, which was current in nineteenth century works of piety, now savors somewhat of the "fifth column."

A layman can scarcely wish to be "a Religious in the world," and, in a sense, he is right. The lay Christian must be in the world as belonging to the world, and not as *not* belonging to it. His "rule" is one adapted to the customs and constantly changing conditions of his daily life, but it is also, in its own way, restrictive, demanding and, on occasion, extremely severe. One sees here one of the difficulties of lay life. God forbid that lay life should have no "rule," but its rule is a contingent one which cannot be determined in advance. Its exercises are flexible exercises which must conform to time available, to temperament, to health, to opportunity. This demands both a great deal of judgment and prudence and a spirit of inventiveness. I have known laymen who learned to use the rhythms and stops of the morning subway to sustain their meditation, just as the sound of the 'Ave' at Lourdes carries the prayer. I have known others who learned to use, on occasion, the darkness of the cinema for a similar purpose; and yet others who cultivated their own moments of solitude when caught up in the waiting lines of "the rush hour." I have known others who transformed their manual labor into a kind of personal liturgy, carrying out the details of their work with the deliberation of a Trappist. There are many such opportunities, and I am surprised that more is not written about them. St. Francis de Sales simplified piety considerably for Philothea, but the simplification consisted especially in shortening the time of her exercises. One can go much further in the same direction. Any more than does love, true piety does not require a lot of time. Those who love know that one can have two trains of thought, one concerned with the work in hand while the other ranges over and finds peace in the object loved; and they also know that, so far from injuring the work in hand, this "ranging" gives it a new quality. In his book, *Jeu*, Patrice de La Tour de Pin shows us this spirit in action:

"The poet goes to the town and spends the whole day there. He sees a railway station, a church, a market. He passes a working man, some boys, a girl, a rich woman reciting her Rosary, a flower-girl who offers him a queen-marguerite saying, 'Here, young man, have a little queen in bloom!' And the poet then reflects that this flower-girl's occupation is like his own: she changes flowers into money, he into poetic language. He too, he reflects, is also like a flower which nature has ordered to make a pattern in the heart of the light. Thus the poet continued his walk, responsive to every chance occurence, his mind disposed and open to the mystery hidden in every created thing, finding there a means of access to God.

"He found himself entering into 'a kind of order' in which he would not recognize even his brothers. Henceforward, I shall be *a wandering contemplative,* in no way vowed to seclusion and continual silence or employed in interpreting the mysteries of God and man in the world, but bound, like all others, to cultivate submission to His Church and humility of mind."

It occurred to me that this poet is the likeness of the layman of the new age, bearing witness where he finds himself, trying, in the midst of his work, his circumstances, his difficulties, to achieve just such a sublimation of every encounter and every event, not in accordance with any preestablished plan, but with the docility of a person who has preserved his sense of wonder. This poet represents at its most pure what each of us should do—seek the Spirit, not after our work or in distraction from our work, but by deeply penetrating that work to the extent of nourishing ourselves, as on a kind of manna, with the Spirit Who dwells in it.

The essential character of the layman, I have said, is to be intimately incorporated in the society of other men, to such an extent that he is individualized only by the accomplishment of what are called "duties," but are better regarded as "services."

Thus, a lay spirituality necessarily places the emphasis on "the duties of one's state in life." The layman should seek his perfection, not in an Office added to his "services" (as would be the recitation of prayers, which is precisely *the duty of his state* for a priest or Religious), but in a spirit of service in its plenitude. The layman is incarnated in his communities—in his family, his profession, his social life. I do not speak here of international society, which is as yet scarcely in existence and of which the layman does not yet feel himself to be a part. Still, the Christian layman cannot be part of his nation and fulfill his duty as a patriot, without feeling that the nation should play its part by contributing to the growth of a larger, international community of peoples. His pattern of life leads the layman to sanctify his natural occupations in his family, in his work, in his civic duties, and these occupations, in our age, are certainly not as simple and regulated as they were formerly. At every moment he meets with irreconcilables, cases of conscience, the questioning of principles, and this often demands acts of initiative and courage for which he himself must take responsibility, since it is a characteristic

of the modern layman that he is sometimes sole judge of
his own case. Then there is his ultimate possible perspective, in a time of revolution, of bearing a Christian witness
which will lead, not as formerly to the honorable death
at the stake or in the arena, but to the agonies of exile or,
at its worst, to the concentration camp and the oven which
is the modern form of the stake. Such is, in fact, the life
of many of the Christian laity in many countries.

This again emphasizes that lay spirituality is that of
the ordinary virtues. We list them, with Aristotle and St.
Thomas, as prudence, fortitude, temperance, justice; and
we add loyalty, fidelity, sincerity, authenticity, assisting
one's neighbor, which are more in the modern style. It is
not just a question of easy things, but it is characteristic
of this lay spirituality that the practice of these easy things
involves one in spite of oneself and can carry one far.
From this viewpoint, the life of St. Theresa of Lisieux is,
more than that of St. Joan of Arc, providentially fitted to
serve as a model for the laity.

Theresa was, of course, not a lay person, but it can be
said that her spirituality was of the lay *type,* as could also
be said of the spirituality of St. Francis de Sales for his
time. The virtues which Theresa advocates are those which
do not need the cloister for their exercise. They are the
natural virtues informed with love. And Theresa was great,
not as St. Joan by doing heroic actions in a natural way,
but by doing natural and simple actions in a heroic manner.
But, here again, contraries are complementary: Joan and
Theresa come together to form the lay spirituality.

Taking this direction, the layman has not to seek far to
find his road to the kingdom of God, for it stretches away
from his very doorstep. This is particularly true of a
troubled age such as ours, when there are so many invitations to disquiet, to anguish, to despair. Lay spirituality

is the counterpoise to those currents called "existential" which are filled with a spirit opposed to the Christian spirit of peace, calm, trust. This does not imply that anguish, disquiet, and the nervous strain of modern life are things foreign to us, but we seek to sanctify and surmount them.

The Liturgy and the Laity

Originally, the Liturgy was in the language of all, for it was the fixed and regular expression of common prayer which at first had been wholly private and lifted on the wave of personal enthusiasm. To avoid the abuses of private inspiration—an inspiration very difficult to control and, anyhow, intermittent—it has become necessary to decide on certain formulas of prayer. These formulas have become incomprehensible to those who do not know the meaning of the Christian languages. They have, therefore, ceased to correspond entirely to their primitive meaning.

Formerly educative of the people and therefore cultural, the Liturgy has become for the people the language of God and no longer the language of men speaking to God. Formerly, it was the great means by which a whole people approached the Mystery. If the people did not understand the dogmas, at least they understood something about the rites which proportioned the divine to their capacity and which were, so to speak, their respiratory organs in that great sea of eternity where we already move and have our being. But the means has changed into an obstacle. The ceremony in the first Cenacle was *seen* by all present as "the breaking of bread"; whereas today the circular Hosts, machine shaped beforehand into individual units, have not the same *visible* significance as that of a family loaf "broken" and distributed by the Father. The *piscina* from which the neophyte emerged, his naked torso glistening with living water, spoke its own message clearly to the people; whereas, our Baptismal fonts say indeed the same thing, but as it were in a whisper. Public penances were also visible instruction; our Confessional "penances" are performed privately.

This change is no matter for surprise. It illustrates a general law of development, of maturation, of continuity, about which we can do nothing. Since the Liturgy is essentially sacred because of its antiquity and of all the holy customs, it is very difficult to modify it. And if, side by side with the sacred Liturgy, we institute a kind of popular liturgy, it will lack consecration.

I find the solution here only in a two-fold effort. The first must come down from the heights; the other must sublimate the depths as much as possible. The ancient Liturgy must be thoroughly explained and interpreted. It is like a movie in a foreign language for which subtitles must be supplied. On the other hand, let us raise the best of our popular hymns to the height of a second liturgy.

This brings me to the problem of the Mass, in which all is resumed and recapitulated. The Mass, originally self-explanatory to the people, is now incomprehensible to the non-initiated. In the "ages of Faith," as they are called, the Mass was no doubt incomprehensible to those who did not know Latin, but as religious instruction came to the people from other sources, all that they knew served to clarify the Mass. Assistance at Mass, though a silent assistance, was the symbol of antecedent Christian life. The milieu being no longer Christian, this is not the pattern of things today. People now only assist at Mass, or at certain Masses—for instance Palm Sunday Mass, Requiem Masses—in the rural districts of France. More than an initiation into, a directing of knowledge towards the rare Masses at which they assist, is necessary in our de-Christianized societies; it would be necessary to impregnate the whole course of the week or year with Christian thought, in an analogous manner to that "antecedent Christian life" we have noted in the Ages of Faith.

The psalms, prayers and readings which precede the Offertory are aimed at explaining to the Christian people what is about to take place, to remind them of the meaning of the Scriptures, and to lead them to renew their faith. It is an admirable mode of instruction, poetic, didactic, symbolic. But now that explanation itself needs to be explained; the people must be initiated into this initiation.

A friend of mine talked to me recently about the essential elements of the Mass and about what he called the "severed" elements. "The dimensions of the Mass," he said, "must be extended to the whole of life. When we *read* in a spirit of prayer, when we chant the psalms or sing hymns in the same spirit, when we study the doctrines of the faith, we are preparing ourselves to understand the Mass. Similarly, when we offer ourselves through our great and small sacrifices, when we join in friendship with others, when we carry out our job or profession in a spirit of liturgy and oblation, we repeat the Mass by anticipation, somewhat in the sense that actors repeat a play. The Mass may be of short duration. It is, in fact, considerably condensed. In this ancient text, there may be errors, omissions, redundancies through repetition, but this is a matter for the archeologists and the liturgists, and scarcely interests me. Whatever words are used in the accomplishment of these mysteries, the words will always be inadequate. What I must grasp is the *meaning*—in other words, the living relationship of this moment of oblation to all the phases of my life.

"The Roman Mass, so soon completed with the *Ite,*

Missa est from which it derives its name, is a summary of human history. It is a micro-history, with its great event, the Consecration, centrally placed and yet enveloping the whole, just as the palm of the hand envelopes the grains of wheat. It is also the image of our individual history. In my view, to explain the Mass would be to make people realize that what they do every day they will find there under real symbols."

The Priest and Christian Homes

There is a sense in which the saying, "No priest between you and me," is perfectly tenable and legitimate. The priest must not be the one who opposes husband to wife or wife to husband, even when this is done for the best of motives. On the contrary, he is bound to help them to live in the highest and most constant unity. He should help the couple to live the grace of their marriage, which is a bond of perfection.

But here we must meet an objection one often hears from our Protestant brethren, that the priest, being unmarried, is incompetent to advise a married couple. This is a fundamental objection, since it raises the question of competence in matters of love.

It is wrong, in these matters, to subordinate intelligence to experience, as if experience were the sole spring of sympathy. I am well aware of the harm that can be done, in the matter of giving advice, by a man of purely scholastic intelligence who knows only about general types and not about particular cases, whose attitude is that life must of necessity produce "cases" exactly like those of the morality "paradigms" of his text books. Perhaps one does meet with certain priests and Religious who have this closed circuit type of mind. But, in these matters, *experience,* in the ordinary sense of the word, is not of itself and of itself alone sufficient, for it is not always governed by conditions which would make it a vital and integral experience.

A meticulous and pure intelligence, which seeks all the facts and reflects deeply on the significance of those facts, which tries to enter sympathetically into everything, is capable of understanding love more fully than is the lover himself. The Curé of Ars certainly knew more about love than did Balzac. St. Francis de Sales, who has written so well about nuptial love, knew nothing about it except as in the light of Divine Love.

A family who lacked the supernaturally inspired friendship of some priest from which to derive strength, would be deprived of an essential prop. This priest-friend need not necessarily be the confessor or director of the couple, or of husband or wife, nor need he be their parish priest or a priest relative, though of course this may be so. To understand this, I must lead my reader to consider the essence itself of conjugal love.

The characteristic proper to conjugal love is that each partner finds self-realization only in the complete giving of self to the other. Each finds himself or herself only by losing himself or herself in the other. Marriage is therefore much more than mere "togetherness" or even a bond. Like unity, like purity, like everything delicate in this world, unity is always under threat. It is threatened by the temptation experienced sooner or later by husband or wife, to lead his or her life autonomously, to enjoy happiness apart. It may even be that there are desertions at a high level, as when one of them has "a mystic garden enclosed" to which the other is not admitted. Unity is also threatened by the sufferings and the cares of life, by family preoccupations, by sickness, by fear, by the absence of generosity and of the spirit of "forgive and forget."

It is in this connection that the priest-friend can play an important role by reminding the couple of the ideal of their married life, an ideal now rendered more beautiful by having been matured in difficulties and trials. Such a priest must bear in mind that, while it is true that soul differs from soul, it is even more true that married couple differs from married couple, for at each marriage a unique constellation is brought into being. As a priest, his function here is thoroughly to know this two-fold constellation, and then to help it to know itself.

I should also like to say something about the absent family collaborator, the Trappist or the Carmelite who not only departs from the family, but can no longer watch the family. It suffices to read the letters of St. Theresa of Lisieux or of Sister Elizabeth of the Trinity, to realize how deeply intimate and how helpful a cloistered soul can be to its own family outside and indeed to all families. The example of one who has renounced family life is of service to love itself. But here, let us listen to Professor Foester, who is a Protestant and whose remarks, therefore, have the authority of witness from an unaccustomed quarter: "Whoever would understand the necessity for the extraordinary sacrifices to which spiritual enthusiasm raises the saints, must remember a deep truth which is hidden behind all great efforts to dominate the world: the fact that, behind all the purest and sweetest natural gifts, there lurks the heaviest of curses for a man's character if he becomes the slave of those gifts instead of preserving his freedom from their obsessive domination. In family life, for example, there is the root of the most delicate human sentiments, but also the danger of familial egoism and in consequence the withering of every kind of noble love

and of all spiritual effort. Hence there must always be
those rich in grace, who are willing to sacrifice not only
what is ugly but also what is in itself beautiful. They do
so, not in order to embitter the things of the earth for
their fellow-men, but to redeem those things from the
abuse, the excesses, the overestimation to which they are
always liable in human hearts."

And he continues:

"People of the type of St. Elizabeth, even when, in the
ardor of their approach to their Savior they shiver the
ordinary framework of family life, are nevertheless and
even by this very fact the guardian angels of the family;
for they bring to family life a spirit of more disinterested
service, a more spiritual solitude, and they preserve it
from that alliance with the baser instincts which brings
about its real dissolution. There is a Hindu proverb, 'As
hungry birds to their mother, so do men press around the
holocaust of the man who has conquered the world.' This
expresses picturesquely how the conqueror of the world
belongs to the world and is indispensable to the world,
and how, in the midst of the tragic difficulties of their
own lives, people aspire to the bliss of being completely
free. This is so and will always be so: men constantly
insult and abuse the supreme good, and at the same time
they obscurely suspect that they cannot get along without
the light and the strength that emanate from it."

The Holy Trinity is surrounded by Angels, as Isaiah
tells us; and the modern family is surrounded by those
who assist it. Here the prophetic words of Father Viollet
are relevant: "It is the celebates who will save the family."
For the sight of conjugal love and of its blessing in children, the sight of this community of life between so many
different and yet very united people, is, as Coventry Pat-
more says, a fountain of virginity, at which religious souls

can ceaselessly refresh themselves. Though it is true that
the Christian family receives great services from their
collaborators, it is equally true that the collaborators receive more than they give.

Finally, it may be said that, in a sense, the priest is
the bond of families. Many in our day feel a desire to have
a new Order. What is an Order, except an adaptation of
the Gospel to the needs of society, under the control of
the Church? The major Religious Orders were and still
are just that, and the Third Orders likewise. But the time
will undoubtedly come when the original rules of the
Orders and Third Orders, drawn up in a triumphant or
militant epoch of Christianity, no longer meet the necessities created in a de-Christianized society. One of the
characteristics of our age—in which the Spirit is as active
as in other ages, though in different ways—is the emergence of fully Christian homes, animated with the spirit
of the Gospel, the fruits of a union which is also regarded
as a vocation. These homes exist here and there like the
cells of a sublime and hidden Order, without 'habits,'
without outward form, without ordination, vows, rule or
cloister, but not without its radiation into society, its influence, its penetration. And the same Spirit Who formerly
made His presence felt in the world—and Who will always
do so for certain privileged souls— by inspiring people to
retire from the contagion of the world, now inspires
certain people to merge themselves in the world to the
point of having no visible mark to distinguish them from
their fellow-men. This attitude is the spirit of Nazareth,
the Marian spirit, the Pauline spirit. In the Middle Ages,
real communication was virtually impossible except among
people who lived together; it is quite different today, when
the Atlantic can be crossed in a few hours.

But what is to be the bond of these families, the tissue

linking these living cells? Who will visit them, look after them, raise them to higher levels, put them in touch with one another? Who will enrich one of these homes with the aspirations and hopes of another of its kind? Who will link them with the Universal Church? Who will assure the passage from the old to the new, from yesterday to today? One sees the role which the priest can here fulfill as servant of this dispersed "Order." He can be, as it were, the chain of gold linking these gold rings, or the unifying pith of these families remote from one another but united by bonds of higher love.

Furthermore, when the union of priest and homes becomes an organic and vital union, it emerges clearly that, on their part, the homes help the priest as much as he helps the homes. We have here something quite distinct from the idea of making the priest a specialist in problems of love, or of introducing him into that conjugal life which should preserve its own secret. After long reticence among Christians concerning sex, there is now a tendency to talk about little else in connection with marriage. This will pass, for physical love is simply the instrument of an oblative dedication. This dedication is a help given to everything which deserves to exist and to develop in the world: family, profession, nation, internation; instruction, growth in holiness, education, mission, Church. The priest's zeal united with the love of these homes, can powerfully nourish this flame.

Towards New Orders

The patriarchal system compelled the newly married to live with the family. The father of the family, the *paterfamilias* of ancient Roman law, was the absolute master of this community. He ruled over his sons and over his son's wives. All new alliances within his family came under his law. Such a regime fitted in well with rural life, for many hands were needed on the farm. We still find in rural countries that the son brings his bride into the home, where she lives with her mother-in-law and her sisters-in-law, who accept her quite easily. For there is much urgent work to do at all times, and they are glad of her help.

That was a strange saying of Christ: "A man shall leave his father and his mother." It implied that a man was juridically freed from attachment to the group, and that, by their marriage, the man and the woman were creating a new home. That is what we see happen now-adays. No doubt, housing shortage still obliges married couples to live with in-laws, but in our day this is scarcely advisable because of the friction it can cause. Whose fault is this? It is hard to say. Experience shows that women who are not of the same blood as the people with whom they live, tend to become irritable and discontent.

More and more, homes in our western world are becoming independent and self-centered units. Love which jealously concentrates on itself loses some of its power by thus turning in on itself. It is also shortsighted, since, in its needs, it cannot obtain help from others, having turned away from all others to draw a tight little circle round itself.

One suggestion would be to group the homes in a pattern of a more voluntary and more flexible kind than that of the old patriarchal system.

I am thinking of a hamlet of which I am at present a very living part. It is in the heart of France, about equidistant from the pole and the equator, from the Ocean and the Alps. Apart from the English during the Hundred Years War, no invasions have touched it. Its way of life has scarcely changed since the neolithic age, when man came to live here on a stony ridge by the banks of a sluggish river. The church is a league away, the railway station four leagues. There is no grocery store or school house in this hamlet, nothing in fact which would *incarnate* the idea of a life led in common. It is simply a community of seven homes.

Relations are as among neighbors, a relationship which is almost extinct in our towns. In Paris, you can live your life without actually knowing your next door neighbor, even if he is a better Christian than yourself. But in the country, especially where there is a group of houses without community links of any kind, the relations are of neighbor with neighbor: mutual help, solidarity, friendship, *agape* in all its forms, are necessary to living. These are, of course, unstable relations, as is everything dependent on feelings; affinities which can be reversed. When this occurs, the "neighborliness" of friendship and mutual assistance quickly changes (and for a generation) into distrust, silence, indifference, a condition aggravated by contiguity.

These groups of houses, always necessitating defense or help, symbolize the spiritual groupings, freed from space and contiguity, which I see coming into being and developing—*the groups of homes.* The Christian homes which are united through mutual aid and *agape* in this arid modern world, are in this way like those settlements of the first human families.

And these groups of dispersed families form a spiritual community, form what was formerly called a religious society, a sodality, a congregation. The name is not important, the essence of the religious association being a communion of people living the same kind of material and spiritual life, with the same purpose of advancing the Kingdom of God.

Up to the present, we have had only religious associations comprised of individuals. To avoid individualism, it was necessary to impose severe rules of obedience, and generally (the individuals being, by definition, without family) to require what is called "the common life." But one can envisage associations which are composed, no longer of individuals, but of homes and families. Such associations would have no material life lived in common, but nevertheless the families who composed them would have analogous patterns of living and convergent pre-occupations. Lawyers' families, families of industrialists, teachers, politicians, agriculturalists, could propose for themselves a common ideal and group themselves into a community of the spirit.

This seems very difficult to organize. In the first place, it is asking people living in the world and at its mercy to exercise the kind of virtues practiced by those who have retired from the world and its temptations. It is true that, in the rude conditions of the past, when, for example, a young girl on her own might well be violated and when no one was sure his house would not be attacked at night, it was wise to take the precaution of stout walls and visible discipline. Furthermore, in the days before the mail, before the telephone, before aircraft, radio and television, it was impossible *to live the same kind of life except when living in the same house.*

We, however, are more autonomous than were our fore-bears. We can have the spirit of discipline and even of intelligent obedience, without being strictly under the command of one superior. For what, fundamentally, is an *Order?* Pascal wrote, "If God gave us commands directly from Himself, how we should obey them with a good heart! We receive them unfailingly from necessity and the events of life"—to which we may add some elements not too familiar to the seventeenth century, such as the duties of our state, the rules of conjugal life, the education of children, the obligations of civic life. These latter "necessities" are still more demanding than commandments and even events of life, for they constantly require from us reflection, responsibility, initiative, solitude.

The Layman and the Idea of Engagement

We must clearly distinguish from one another, the *prophet* and the *priest*, for no good can come from confusing the two ideas. The layman must not be a priest *manqué* or a layman with a priest's mentality.

In the eyes of an indifferent world, the layman, especially if he lives a celebate life, will always appear, of course, a "Religious in disguise." How many devout women there are who are suspect in just this way! It is interesting that persecuting dictators and governments prefer Bishops, priests and religious, to these elusive laymen and laywomen who are indistinguishable from others in the crowd. It is easier to supervise and to persecute the cleric, for he can be known and recognized. We can even find the situation where the atheist State hypocritically honors the Clergy and grinds down the laity, because the priests represent for them the institutional religion which must be allowed to continue and burn itself out, whereas they regard the apostolic layman as representing the living, argumentative, need-conquering, religion which must be overthrown.

What is very new is that there can be apostles who are not priests. This idea was inconceivable in the past when it was taken for granted that the layman should confine himself to the practice of his religion, missionary work being reserved to the Clergy. Therefore, with the assent of both Church and State, the Catholic professional man did not concern himself with testifying to his religion. Formerly such a thing as an "association of Catholic University Professors" would not have been regarded as possible.

———

Theology, it must be emphasized, is a science, and cannot therefore be learned in a day. Like any other science, it demands aptitude, teachers, study, incessant application. The laity are sometimes under the curious delusion, a mixture of suspicion and of secret conceit, that it is enough to have a certain amount of intuition, to indulge in some rather desultory discussion, to read a few books about religion, and presto one is a theologian! They think that theology does not need a technical language, that it can be conveyed in essays, in polemics, in poetry. Of course, they would not entertain such an idea about any of the secular sciences—about geology or atomic physics, for instance. Only theology, they think, is exempted from the laws of aptitude, apprenticeship, systematic and prolonged study.

On the other hand, however, there is a strong tendency on the part of the professional theologian to regard as *an intrusion* the layman's entry into his jealously guarded domain. He concedes with bad grace that the layman has a right to have new ideas and fresh methods, to express himself on religious topics, to have his school and his public, as had Clement of Alexandria. The professional theologian dismisses such a one as "merely an apologist," in other words as a kind of usher whose task is to awaken unbelievers from their torpor and to bring forward some by St. Peter or Tertullian or Pascal, is indeed the principal proselytes. To such a layman the somewhat "ordinary" task is allowed of proving the truth of religion to unbelievers.

All this is paradoxical, because *apology* as understood study—the one which concerns the *foundations*, the real motives. What would become of theology without these foundations? This habit of labeling as "apologist" the lay writer who concerns himself with fundamentals—I have often had to endure it myself—indicates that the theologian has an uneasy conscience. He does not despise the layman; rather he would seek to honor him, as the general honors the soldier in the front line.

———

A very different attitude exists today among some of the laity and some Religious: the attitude which defines the layman in terms of "engagement." We generally meet the word as political engagement in the sense of the historical dialectic such as it is supposed to be. As one correspondent writes, "The layman is the one who is caught up in the struggle to build the city, and not just in the plan of ecclesial structures." By "engagement" some understand a revolt against the established order, an aspiration towards freedom. In this perspective, the layman would become the man in holy revolt, the good Christian who is an honest rebel. And, after all, why not?

At the end of the Middle Ages, the mendicant Friar, Dominican or Franciscan, was a "cathare" loyal to the Holy See. So too, the 20th century layman would have the prophetic vocation—a vocation which has always contained the element of protest, though in his case too the protest would be a loyal and submissive one. In France, there have been some fine examples of this kind of layman. One need only recall two such talented and dissimilar people as Léon Bloy and Bernanos.

But are there others besides these 'loyal protestors'? It may be supposed that, while some laymen are engaged in defending certain parts of the truth, others are devoting themselves to illustrating the whole truth. Some may prefer the whole to the parts, synthesis to analysis, conciliation to conflict. In the lay house, there are many mansions.

Formerly, this unifying function belonged to the theologians; and it must always be, after some fashion, a logician of God who takes up his abode in the solitude of synthesis, in the summit of that pyramid where the wind blows from the deserts. Some day, if the theologian-clerics have neglected to familiarize themselves with the historical, scientific and human data which the moderns are exploring more and more; if they attempt to place the pyramidal point on ancient, eroded rocks they have failed to restore and renew—then it may well be the laity of the 21st century who take up the task of presenting the Whole.

Whatever about this obscure future, a healthy emulation can certainly exist between the Clergy and the laity. It must be remembered that the role of consecration of the creation, the real *poièsis* (of which poetry is simply a literary species) belongs to all Christians; but it is especially the office of those whose professional occupation is with the cosmos and with history.

And it is here that the word *Prophet*, so dear to Newman, takes on its full meaning. The prophet is the man of God; he is also the man who closely attends, not to the abstract dialectic of history so dear to the false prophets,

but to the real, ever new, never predictible movement of
divine and human history. Plunged in time, nourished by
its mystery, the prophet considers each day in the light
of eternity, that he may strive to utter the truth most
needed for that day.

7

Last Thoughts

The Laity in the World of Tomorrow

If Newman presented in a very sunny light the office of
the laity in the Church, this was not solely through a
memory of times past, nor because of his philosophy of
conscience, nor because of his theology of prophetism.
Himself a prophet in his time, he foresaw that the Church
was on the threshold of a period in which she would be
confronted by a learned and cultural atheism, and in
which she would need competent defenders, who would
come for the most part from the ranks of the laity.

After 1880, the Cardinal's attention was caught by the
dangers which attacks against the Bible would create for
the rising generation. Despite his advanced age, Newman
formed the project of going to Rome to speak to Leo XIII
about the new forms which Catholic education should
take. Sickness prevented him from carrying out this idea.
But one day, towards the end of his life, he asked himself
(jokingly, no doubt) what would happen in the very
unlikely event of his being elected Pope. He reminded
the friends with whom he was conversing about one Pope
who, although elected at ninety-three years of age and

dead at ninety-six, nevertheless succeeded in making, during those few years, important decisions for the Church. Then he went on to say that his first act would be to appoint a commission of learned men with a mandate to compare the conclusions of science with the data of traditional teaching, with regard to the Biblical question and the history of Christian origins.

Newman came to believe that, in the future, the world would concentrate around two poles, that of the conscious atheists and that of the convinced Catholics, the intermediary positions having ceased to exercise a profound influence. He saw prophetically what we now see coming about in our own time with the worldwide spread of Marxism—atheism founded on the sciences and on technology. He saw clearly that, if God were to be denied, Catholicism would immediately lose its basis. "I am a Catholic by virtue of my believing in God," he wrote in his *Apologia*. And at the same time he would consider all the apparent power of modern atheism.

In 1839, in his Oxford sermons, Newman raised the question whether atheism was not philosophically in accord with the phenomena of the physical world considered in themselves. In 1875, he gave as his opinion that, of all the matters of faith, the existence of God is the one surrounded with the greatest difficulties, and yet the one which imposes itself on our minds with the greatest force. He went on to remark that in his time "reason" was tending towards disbelief. His friendship with William Froude, Mark Pattison, Blanco, White—all sincere unbelievers—had led him to conclude that there are intelligent people for whom Christianity, in the form in which it is presented to them, is unassimilable. In moments of weariness, he foresaw the time when a new deluge would cover the world, with only a few rare peaks left unsubmerged;

when men would believe in atheism before discovering
Revelation. Old age did not make him more optimistic.
He sensed that a time was coming when the vast majority
of mankind would take it for granted that Christianity had
been refuted and was now outmoded, and who would
scorn to argue with those who obstinately clung to their
belief.

What Russian Marxism finds most difficult is not the
conquering of the Western World: brute force could
achieve that. The difficult task will be to absorb Catholicism. Ultimately, the conflict will be between these two
poles. The choice will present itself, as Newman foresaw,
between radical atheism and the least accommodated or
accommodating religion; between the philosophy which
denies most and the philosophy which affirms most and
which thereby also demands most.

An extract from one of his letters sums up Newman's
ideas about an approach to this subject: "So far as I can
see, there are ecclesiastics all over Europe, whose policy
it is to keep the laity at arms-length, and hence the laity
have been disgusted and become infidel, and only two
parties exist, both ultras in opposing directions.... You
will be doing the greatest possible benefit to the Catholic
cause all over the world, if you succeed in making the
University a middle station at which laity and clergy can
meet, so as to learn to understand and to yield to each
other, and from this, as from a common ground, they
may act in union upon an age which is running headlong
into infidelity...." (Quoted Ward: Vol. II, pp. 397-398).

––––––

In the absence of religious teaching well suited and
extended to all, the majority of the religious peoples of

the world have a faith based on habit and actuated by the pull of custom. How many laity of former times could have answered their adversary, as St. Peter desired, by giving an account of the faith that was in them?

In an age when, even in Asia and Africa, universal education has turned the average man into a reasoning person, eager to know why he acts, why he should believe, we witness an ever increasing *need to understand* which upbringing and custom can no longer satisfy. This emphasis on thinking is a good thing, and should be respected; an effort should be made to end the deviation between secular knowledge and religious ignorance which exists at the national level as well as in the minds even of those who regard themselves as well educated. It is within this gulf that the layman must work, in order in some degree to lessen it.

The passage from routine conformity to intelligent acting, or, as Newman puts it, from *material faith* to *formal faith*, cannot occur within the space of one generation: the development of consciousness is much slower than that of life and technique. Yet as aiding this development, the layman is indispensable. We may say that the disbelief, which today seems to be extending and thickening, is a transitory phenomenon. The more a man is freed from the grind of work and given more leisure, the more he will think about fundamental questions. Then it may well be that an immense religious need will awaken in a world arid of God and aware of the absurdity of existence if there is no God. Despair may be the solution of some of the literati; it will never be the religion of the masses, who will not remain forever in the grip of atheism. But, in order to obtain this awakening to salvation, a much greater effort must be made to offer religion *to men's intelligence,* so that it does not appear as something contrary to that scientific development which is the wonder of our times.

Therefore, as Newman saw, it will not be a question of announcing the Gospel, but of re-announcing it to those who have known and then abandoned it, believing that they themselves have weighed it in the balance and found it wanting. This mission to reconvert is more difficult than the mission to convert. There is no longer the effect of surprise. The kerygmatic announcing of the faith to a people that have lost it must occur from person to person, village by village. Each small group, each educated family, each community, has already become a highly alert and intellectually demanding mental world. It must be *re-evangelized*. Every layman must be able to give an account to his fellow workers *of the hope that is in him.* And this demands a deep knowledge of fundamental matters, and an adaptation to the modern way of thought. It demands long continued perseverance in light and in love: results come slowly, like the maturing seed, when one is dealing with the few, who listen with but half their attention.

As yet, we have no good guide to these methods of re-conversion. It is here that, following Newman, I regard the lay vocation as having its special place. The layman is called to take his place among the apostles of "these latter times" which will perhaps prove to be the longest period of history.

———

Newman, who is often regarded as the theologian of *evolution*, was on the contrary an upholder of *identity*.

His theory of *development* is not a doctrine concerning changes in the Faith in the course of history, but on the contrary a doctrine of its fundamental and abiding *identity*: "the unity and identity of the idea with itself through all stages of its development from first to last." (*Development*, p. 206). Newman could have applied Leibniz's words to the Church, that "everything is always the same, almost to degrees of perfection"—i.e., in his context, almost to the same degrees of explicitness. In each epoch of the life of that living organism, the Church, there is the same equilibrium between the parts, the same equivalence of forces present.

Newman gives some examples of this equivalence. Thus, he says, each age has its special character: that of the Fathers was contemplative and mystical; ours is more practical. Any historian would admit that there have been changes in the moral condition and in what could be called the mentality of the Church. But it is remarkable that there is always an equivalence (an "intimate connection, or rather oneness"—*Development* p. 169) between these diverse epochs, these diverse phases of the life of the Church. Tendencies and fundamental requirements are equally satisfied, although the manner of doing so varies. Thus the cult of Tradition is not a matter of *literal* fidelity to the pattern of antiquity. In the societies of this world, identity of external aspects at all times often indicates very insipid associations. "An idea does not always bear about it the same external image; this circumstance, however, has no force to weaken the argument for its substantial identity, as drawn from its external sameness, when such sameness remains. On the contrary, for that very reason, *unity of type* becomes so much the surer guarantee of the healthiness and soundness of developments, when it is persistently preserved in spite of their number and importance." (*Development*, p. 178).

One and the same truth, Newman points out, can be expressed in a variety of languages and images. We see this in Mathematics, where the same relationships can be expressed in the language of geometry or in that of algebra. In the sciences, truths belonging to one province of knowledge are currently used to express truths of a neighboring province: thus rhetoric is simply the transposition of reasoning into the language of the emotions. This law is found in the history of Christianity. The doctrine of "justification by faith" is, in Newman's view, the form under which the Reformation sought to interpret Catholic belief in the efficacy of Baptism. And the taste for religious poetry fulfilled in the nineteenth century the office of the contemplative spirit which was so powerful among the Fathers.

Aided by this view of the *equivalence* of the ages, one could perhaps re-think the position of the modern laity. It should also be remembered that the age at hand (which will express in its own way the identity of the Church with herself), will be the age in which the ecclesiastical community will be more *one* in which the people will be nearer to their Bishop, the Pope to his faithful, the laity to their Clergy; and that this emergence of the laity, grown to adult age in the Church of tomorrow, will compensate for what the Church may have lost in social power. For the laity, then become more of "apostles" and "prophets," will be able to supply for the shortage of priests to do catechetical work. What the Church loses in quantity, she will gain in quality. Quantity is justified only if it implies increase of quality.

The masses and the *élite* are the two zones which, despite appearances, are always nearest to Catholic plenitude. *The masses,* because Catholicism is designed for the multitude; it is the most "universalizable" religion, the one most capable of uniting the learned and the unlearned, the form of religious life which, without compromising with weakness, takes most account of the real conditions of religion for the multitude. *The élite*, because, to be fully understood intellectually, Catholicism demands an effort of synthesis which challenges the highest capacities of the human mind.

APPENDIX

Clergy and Laity in the Early Church

In a recently published history book, this is what the author writes under the heading *Clergy and Laity*:

"Originally any of the faithful was regarded as competent to administer Baptism and to consecrate the Eucharistic bread and wine. Gradually [1] it came to be understood that this was the office proper to the Clergy (Greek *kleros* from *kleroo*, 'to choose by lot,' and generally, 'to choose') who constituted the *ordo clericalis* into which one entered by a special ceremony (*ordination*) and thereby became distinguished from laity (from *laos*, the people). There

1. It seems that this "gradually" unduly extends the origins of the Clergy, for the text suggests that the Clergy (klerikoi) were at a very early period distinct from the Christian people (laos). It is certainly beyond doubt that those whom we call "the Clergy" were, from the beginning, distinct from the simple laity. But we do not find in any of the Apostolic Fathers that the members of the clergy were called *clerici*. According to Eusebius (V, 28, 12), it was under Zepherinus (early third century) that this name was introduced. The First Epistle of St. Peter (V, 1-3) uses *kleros* to indicate the group of faithful people entrusted to a "presbyter" or Bishop, in the same sense in which St. Paul speaks of his canon (2 *Cor.*, X, 16), that is to say, of the "lot" which has been given to him (*Rom.*, XV, 20).

are now, therefore, two categories of Christians, one active, the other almost passive, in the Church."

Of course, this work is a summary for use in schools, and its author had not space enough to cite his sources. But this problem of the distinction between Clergy and laity is more than just a little matter of history, for it raises the important question: What is the origin of authority in the Church? Is this authority an emanation from the community of the faithful or a delegation from Heaven? Does it reside in the Christian people or in the body of the pastors?

It is more useful than ever to consider this subject, because those among our separated brethren who are attracted by the example of our faith, have not always a clear idea of how the part of the layman and that of the priest are understood in the Church of Christ.

First, we shall discuss how the power of Baptism was transmitted in the Church. This will throw light on the transmission of the power to consecrate. These two Sacraments are at the heart of the life of the Church, since Baptism gives grace and the Eucharist maintains and develops that grace to the highest degree. When these two points have been clarified, the role of the laity in the Church can be discerned.

A. Baptism

1. Christ instituted, if not the *rite*, at least the *necessity* of Baptism, when He solemnly declared that no one can enter into the invisible kingdom of heaven except through that visible kingdom of God which is the Church (Matt., X, 14, 15; XI, 20-24; Mk., VI, 11; Lk., IX, 5). But how is one introduced into this visible society? Clearly, this must be through a solemn ceremony performed by compe-

tent authority before witnesses. In a sense, this is analogous to the process by which an alien becomes a naturalized citizen; the Baptismal rite gives one "citizenship rights" in the celestial city. Baptism cannot be repeated, for a conditional giving of ourselves to God would be an outrage against His sovereign majesty. Hence the necessity for a new intervention of authority to reconcile the Christian with God, if that Christian has violated his promise by official and flagrant heresy or schism, by public and notorious scandal, or by his private conduct. It is thus that the Sacrament of Penance makes its appearance in the economy of Divine Providence as the natural complement of the Baptismal invitation.[2]

2. We do not find in the *Acts* or in the writings of the Apostles that any layman ever conferred Baptism.

Peter himself baptized or saw to the Baptism of all the Jewish converts at Jerusalem (*Acts*, II, 41), and Peter and John, representing the college of the Twelve, admitted into the Church the Samaritans, by completing the work of Philip who had "preached to them about God's kingdom" (*Acts*, VIII, 14-17). But, as "God's kingdom" was daily increasing, the right to introduce into the Church had to be delegated for remote countries. This delegation was made to great missionaries or evangelizers not belonging to the Twelve, and St. Paul designates these as Apostles (1 *Cor.*, XV, 7; 2 *Cor.*, XI, 13)[3]

To these apostles of the second plane, we can add the deacon Philip (*Acts*, VI, 5) who surpassed them through the prestige of his apostolate among the Samaritans, so

2. This complement is necessary only for those who have violated the engagements entered into at their Baptism (11 *Cor.*, XI, 13).

3. If the Twelve only had been called apostles, it would never have occurred to St. Paul to warn the faithful against impostors "disguised as apostles of Christ," for their pretence would have been self-evident.

fruitful in conversions and in miracles. (*Acts,* VIII, 5-14). In this chapter of the *Acts* (VIII, 39) we read that Philip conferred Baptism on "courtier of Candace, queen of Ethiopia." But here it must be borne in mind:

(a) that Philip is a deacon, meaning that he has received *the imposition of hands* which has made him a sacred minister of inferior rank (*Acts,* VI, 6);

(b) that the work of Philip was not perfected until "the apostles began to lay their hands on them, so that the Holy Spirit was given them" (*Acts,* VIII, 17).

Christian initiation then comprised both ablution and the imposition of hands.

The imposition of hands was the privilege of the higher authority of the Twelve, and the ablution was to be carried out by the ministers of the Twelve, and the ablution was to be carried out by the ministers of the second order. Thus we find that only in exceptional cases did Paul himself baptize at Corinth (1 *Cor.,* I, 14-16); in most cases, he left it to his assistants to administer the rite of Baptism, while he devoted himself entirely to the preaching of the word (*ibid.,* 17-18). However, the ablution, then as now, was of itself necessary and sufficient to give "citizenship rights" in the Church, as is shown by the case of Philip and the eunuch of Queen Candace.[4]

3. If the Church now allows the laity to confer Baptism on children in danger of death—this Sacrament, according to St. John (111, 5), alone assuring entry into Heaven—she regards the lay person who baptizes as endowed with an implicit delegation. Baptism conferred by a lay person

4. The development of the Sacraments has accentuated the original separation between Baptism and Confirmation but without altering their essential character. It would be a serious error to belittle Confirmation which is the perfecting of the Christian initiation secured by Baptism; but Confirmation is not indispensable to the makng of a Christian.

on a child who has not reached the age of reason, is recognized by the Church, if it has been administered in accordance with the prescribed forms and conditions. Here there is no question of deciding aptitude to administer; Christ is always ready to admit into His Mystical Body any person *having the proper dispositions* (1 *Cor.*, XII, 26-27) and who comes to him (*John*, VI, 37).

B. *The Eucharist*

The question we raise concerning the Eucharist is twofold:

(1) Did Christ give to His Apostles the power to consecrate the Eucharist?

(2) Did the Apostles give to the faithful the power to consecrate, which they received from Christ?

We shall consider each in turn.

(1) It is clear that if the Christian Eucharist were merely a symbol and not also a reality, its consecration would be merely the blessing of a meal regarded as a sacred repast, and any of the faithful would be capable of accomplishing it, especially if he represented the community and had been delegated to do so by the community.

But since this consecration changes the very substance of bread and wine into the Body and Blood of Christ, the consecrator must have a power which Christ alone could give and which the consecrator must have received by successive, unbroken transmission. Now, it was to the Twelve and to them *alone*, representing by their mystical number the universal body of pastors, that Christ confided this power at the Last Supper (*Lk.*, XXII, 19; 1 *Cor.*, XI, 24-25). It is they whom He charged to govern the Church and to continue the sacrifice which He had begun on the

Cross and which He continues in Heaven and on the Altar (*Heb.*, VII, 24-25).

(2) Did the Apostles transmit this power?

In the first place, the power was transmissible because the Twelve were numerically insufficient to consecrate the Eucharist in every part of the ever extending Church of Christ, and, since they were subject to death, this power would have disappeared with them had it not been communicable. Now, there is no evidence that the Apostles transmitted to the faithful, in a general and irrevocable manner, the power which Christ had given them to consecrate the Eucharist. Indeed there are two texts which suggest the contrary:

(a) In the *Didache*, written between the first and second centuries but more probably at the end of the first, the faithful chose the Bishops and deacons who would carry out for them the ministry of the prophets (XV)—in other words, preach and consecrate the Eucharist, as is indicated earlier in the same document (X). But the whole question is: What was meant here by choosing? Does it signify *power*, or does it merely signify the choosing of someone *fitted to receive* such power?

(b) The epistle of St. Clement of Rome to the Corinthians (c. 97) throws great light on this matter. (XI-IV).

According to an apostolic rule (consequently, a rule inspired by the ideas of Christ and universally received), the Bishop-priests *established* at Corinth by the Apostles ought, after their death, to be replaced by those whom, *with the consent of the Church, wise men of high esteem* (*èllogímōn andron*) were to choose and *establish* (katasthaténtas).

What, then, did the community do at the end of the first century? It approved; it agreed. The offices filled by the founder apostles of the churches were henceforth held by "wise men of high esteem" who established the ministers. Now, these ministers, according to St. Clement, "offered the gifts"—the usual expression of the time for consecrating the Eucharist. According to the Didache itself, the Eucharist is a sacrifice and the *only* sacrifice used in the Church (XIV).

But who were the "wise men of high esteem"? And did they not, in their turn, receive from the community the power to elect? History alone can provide the answer, and history shows that very soon, and probably at a very early stage, they were the Bishops of neighboring churches. The Council of Nicaea, in the fourth Canon, was to make this the law for the whole Church. St. Cyprian tells us that, towards 257, this usage was almost universal, that it was of apostolic origin and that it was even "of divine tradition." [5]

An indirect proof adding weight to these direct ones, is the absence of any evidence to support this supposed deposition of the laity. According to our author, everyone would have been a priest at the very early period of the Church. The suppresson of this, had such a situation been there in the first place, would have created a serious crisis within the Church, and this would certainly have left its traces, at least in some churches. The laity would not without protest have allowed themselves to be deprived of a privilege which they would have regarded as held from the Apostles and therefore from Christ. The first Christian authors, such as Sts. Clement, Ignatius and Polycarp, have recorded less serious and more local crises. Now, for these

5. Ep. LXIII, 5, P.L., tome III, col. 1057. This expression must be understood in a very general sense, for we do not find in the New Testament that Christ ever exactly prescribed for his Apostles how they were to choose their successors.

saintly Bishops and martyrs, the hierarchy of Bishops, priests and deacons was willed by Christ, and the letters in which they proclaimed this tradition were always received with respect by the faithful. Thus, about the year 110, St. Ignatius of Antioch warns the Smyrniotes against ascetics who were abstaining from the Eucharist (VII, 1) or at least were celebrating it apart without the participation of authority. "Never do anything which concerns the Church, without the Bishop. Regard as lawful only the Eucharist celebrated with the Bishop or his delegate presiding" (*Smyrniotes*, VIII, 1).[6]

C. The Role of the Laity in the Church

We have seen that the Catholic Church was established by Christ as a visible society in submission to an authority which she did not give to herself but which she received directly from Christ (*Matt.*, XVIII, 18-20); that this authority was extended by subordination and by delegation, in space and in time, without ever becoming detached from its transcendent Head Who assists it always (*ibid.*, 20; *Heb.*, XIII, 8); that this implies, in its origins, a clear cut distinction between the Hierarchy and the Christian

6. There were schisms in the churches to which Ignatius was writing, and it is possible that some priests had been involved and were continuing to celebrate the Eucharist. Later, in the time of St. Cyprian, there was even a woman who consecrated the Eucharist and involved in her schism a priest and a deacon (P.L., tome III, col. 1215). Of course, the sacerdotal character cannot be abolished, and the words pronounced by the heretic priest over the bread and wine have their full effect; but this Eucharist, though valid is not licit, and the faithful who knowingly take part in it put themselves outside the body of the Church. This was how St. Ignatius regarded the matter, and this has always been the attitude of the Church.

people, the Church teaching and the Church taught, the shepherd and his flock (*Mk.*, 111, 19).

This being the case, should we not say that the laity were reduced to *a passive role* and that they relinquished their religious personality into the hands of a prying authority? To answer this, let us first attempt to clarify two points:

(1) The extent to which the layman is subject to authority;

(2) The extent to which the layman can help in the sanctification of the Church.

(1) To what acts is the layman bound vis-à-vis religious authority?

There are only two Sacraments imposed on all the faithful: that of the initiation or *Baptism-Confirmation* and that of Communion or the *Eucharist*. The obligation of Baptism—which is one with the rational obligation to enter the Church when one has come to know it—affects you once in life; that of the Eucharist, once a year. The natural contract which creates husband and wife becomes the Sacrament of Matrimony when it takes place between Christians, and, since the Council of Trent, it must be contracted in the presence of the due religious authority to be recognized by the Church, just as in some places it must take place in the presence of the civil authority to be recognized by the State. The Sacraments of *Penance* and *Extreme Unction* are necessary for salvation only if one has culpably put oneself outside the Church by serious infringement of the Moral Law. Finally, there is our obligation to assist at Sunday Mass if we can do so, as we see to have been the practice from earliest times among the faithful in both town and country (*Justin*, First Apology, LXVII). The authority of the Church limits its intervention, therefore, in our lives, to *a minimum* of precepts necessary to the Christian life which we profess. Of course, the Church earnestly counsels us to frequent Confession and Communion which abundantly apply to our souls the fruits of the Redemption and efficaciously help us to fulfill the natural moral law (*Mk.*, X, 19-20). But a careful distinction must be made between *precept* and *counsel* (*ibid.*, 21; cf. *Matt.*, XIX, 21) if we are to mark the limits of our human liberty. These limits coincide with those imposed on us by our reason itself, once it has recognized that entry into the Church is the necessary condition of salvation. (*Matt.*, X, 13-15; *Mk.*, VI, 11; *Lk.*, IX, 5; *Acts*, V, 11).

(2) But while the independence of the layman towards the Church is complete within these limits, it cannot exist in relation to Christ Who is the Head of the Mystical Body of the Church (*Eph.*, 1, 22-23), and Who proposes to all the faithful, lay or clerical, the same ideal of perfection (*Matt.*, V, 48; *Mk.*, X, 21). The layman is a member of the Mystical Body (1 *Cor.*, X, 17) and he can offer up the "spiritual sacrifice," for he belongs, in a sense, as St. Peter tells him, to "a holy priesthood" (1 *Pet.*, 11, 6). These spiritual sacrifices are not the exterior sacrifices celebrated by the priest in fulfillment of his "public office" (*Acts*, XIII, 2; Cf. *Rom.*, XIII, 6), but the sacrifices which are accomplished in the depths of the heart (Ps. LI, 19-20). They are what give a man his true value in the eyes of God, and without which the reception of the Sacraments by the faithful, as the administration of the Sacraments by the priest, would be of little weight for our salvation. This ecclesiastical work of sanctification is carried out between the soul and its Creator—between what Newman calls "the only two supreme and luminously self-evident beings, myself and my Creator" (*Apologia*, ch. 111). And this needs no human intermediary.

Conclusion

We have criticized here a certain evolutionist conception which would see the history of the Church as a series of secret metamorphoses hidden under a nominal unity. If such a façade has survived to cover so many changes, this can only have been through the power exerted by an authority deaf to the demands of new ages—an authority which hinders the progress of free research and which, by isolating traditions in order to conserve them, causes those traditions to become exhausted. Hence it is that, in the history of the Church, authority in every epoch occupies the terrain which life deserts.—*Such is the hypothesis* and at least it is an ingenious one. But if it is applied to history, and especially to the history of the Eucharist to which our investigation here is confined, one must conclude to a "sudden mutation" contrary to everything that tradition reveals and to everything that the ancient texts expressly suggest. Of course, there are gaps in the history, and the documents of the early centuries do not supply answers to all our questions. Have we any right to fill in these gaps with our deductions? Fragile and vain indeed would be a thesis whose only support was the exegesis of some silences.

Let us leave, therefore, these disputes and remain in that domain of living souls into which they have led us. This sketchy account may serve to clarify the Catholic conception of authority by showing how it takes the form that promotes the good of every person.

This authority, indeed, is necessary not only to the exterior discipline of the Church and to the Church's continuity in time, but also to its deeper life which is the building up of Christ in souls. Authority is concerned with the deposit of Revelation. (2 *Tim.*, 1, 14), and where authority has totally failed, as in the Protestant confessions, we see the majority of the dogmatic truths inevitably disappearing. Now, these truths condition to its profoundest depths our entire Christian life. In these pages we have shown how the Divinity of Christ enables us to believe in the reality of the Eucharist and in its efficacy, as well as in the reality and efficacy of Baptism, and how it obliges us to receive His Sacraments, in order that grace may be born and nurtured to growth in the faithful soul, according to the plan of God (*Eph.*, 1, 3-14).